WHAT WILL YOU HAVE?

by

JAMES A. DECKER

"What will you have? quoth God;
pay for it and take it."

NITY BOOKS • UNITY VILLAGE, MO.

Contents

How to Play God

Sometimes we hear it said of someone that he tried to "play god." Invariably the words are spoken critically, usually of one who tried, unsuccessfully, to manipulate the lives and affairs of others, or to bring his own world around to his own way of thinking. The very fact that the thought of playing god has a distasteful connotation for most people emphasizes the misconception many people have of God.

And what an uncomplimentary conception it is! If you have ever spoken, critically, about someone who tried to play god and got into trouble because of it, you have unconsciously

5

held an image of God as One who deliberately manipulates and moves the affairs of His children—One who repeatedly interferes in the lives of men.

If we agree that God is the universal power of good, available whenever and wherever man wants to contact Him, if we agree that His prime gift to man is freedom to make his own choices and decisions, then we can hardly accept the notion of God as interference, manipulation, arbitrary authority, and the like.

Even if we turn to the familiar conventional explanation that "God knows best" to excuse what seem to be unhappy experiences in life, we are not on much firmer ground. It may be comforting to hold this thought to explain away trouble, disaster, and the like; but it is a far cry from the logical truth that God, being all good, cannot send punishing experiences to "teach us a lesson."

All right, you and I are agreed on the nature of God, on our individual freedom as human beings to obey or disobey God's laws. We are agreed that anything unpleasant that confronts us is not "sent from God" as a means of instruction or discipline. So, let's

6

proceed to a firm understanding of our place in God's universal plan.

The Psalmist says without equivocation, "You are gods, sons of the Most High, all of you." And Jesus, criticized for blasphemy, "because you, being a man, make yourself God," quoted the Psalmist, mentioning that he "called them gods to whom the word of God came (and scripture cannot be broken)."

Now admittedly, this is a controversial point. It is a bit difficult for the average man, aware of his apparent inadequacies and failures, to think of himself as a god, even when he knows that Jesus Christ gave full authority to the words and the idea. It seems somehow pretentious for me to think of myself as a god, when I think of how unworthy I am, how many things I do wrong, how often I fall short of my best. But that is the core of the matter: I am not unworthy. If I deny my unworthiness, then I begin to play god, to be the god Jesus Christ says I am, and my errors become fewer and fewer, my successes outweigh my temporary failures.

So you see, the best thing we can do—the very thing we must do, if we want more good—is to play god.

7

In other words, we *are* gods, but we have to act like gods before we can achieve the results we want.

God in us is all-power. But how much does this mean until we believe in the reality of our God-power, believe enough to make ourselves channels for its action?

Marcus Bach says: "Believing in a good fate rather than in a capricious destiny is an achievement so profound that few have ever grasped the total power of it. Believing in courage more than in fear, explorers have discovered and conquered new worlds. Trusting in their abilities, although seemingly defeated, individuals have risen from failure to success; changing from negative to positive thoughts has caused lives to be remade and new careers to come into being."

Every person who has found healing or material success or a genuinely happy way of life has played god. He has taken charge of his life; he has let his God-power govern his affairs.

Here is a woman, troubled with arthritis in the knee; doctor's treatments provide no relief. So she plays god; she begins affirming health, and she asks for prayers. Within three days she is healed. She joins a hiking club and takes weekly hikes lasting several hours. She is 77 years of age, but she had such a strong belief in the God-power within her that she found healing.

Here is another woman, whose daughter is rushed to the hospital, seriously ill. The daughter is not expected to live through the night. (Later the doctor tells the mother: "If I had been a gambler I would not have risked one dollar against three hundred on the possibility of her recovery. The intern and I spent 18 hours of hopelessness, and as time went on there were no hopeful signs.")

But the mother decided to play god, to turn to the God-power within herself. She refuses to accept the medical verdict of "no hope." She prays, believing, in the hospital room and at home. The daughter makes a complete recovery and is at home within a few days.

The mother related all this to us more than ten years later, and there has been no recurrence or further trouble for the daughter in all that time.

Here is a nine-year-old boy who has a large, painful wart on one finger. His father tells him: "Son, if you have enough faith, you know God will remove that wart." So the boy plays god; he goes into another room, with a younger brother, and prays.

When they come out, he says: "God heard me pray. He is going to remove the wart because He said He would, and I know He will." Four days later the wart is gone, and there is never any further sign of it.

Oh, yes, the wart might have disappeared without prayer, either then or later. The actual healing was—as all healings are—a matter of right physical adjustment, a matter of letting the universal law of health and wholeness operate. But the boy himself took the step that made the law operative: he played god, by knowing without any doubt that God's will for him was healing.

You have never seen nor heard of a successful man in any walk of life who didn't possess some kind of strong faith: faith in his ideas, faith in his knowledge, faith in his luck, faith in a circumstance, faith in something. The man who has faith is playing god, whether he knows it or not. He is consciously or unconsciously affirming his steadfast belief in the God-power, the power of good, at work in his life. And when he does this, he leaves himself no time for doubt or recriminations.

Here is one of the most successful career consultants in the country, telling an interviewer: "There were some things I did well, some things I did badly. Altogether I've worked in 187 different fields. But I've had no bad experiences. If I had my life to live over, I wouldn't change it in any way. From every experience I learned something."

Here is a businessman facing an apparently hopeless business situation. Costs are rising, income is decreasing. He begins to take time to think about his employees, and to bless them, consciously and deliberately. Soon they are producing twice as much work! Eventually his employees increase production to such an extent that the employer saves thousands of dollars on a single transaction. He has played god, using his own God-power to bless others, just as we think of God's doing.

Here is a successful automobile dealer who, having been healed of alcoholism through prayer, reasons that "if God could keep him sober, certainly He could help him run an automobile business." The dealer sits down and writes out a contract with God, and he

11

keeps the contract in force.

Now his yearly sales are at the four-million-dollar mark. The dealer says: "One gives happiness and gets back happiness. Create happiness for someone else and happiness automatically becomes yours, never the reverse. You must give peace of mind to get peace of mind."

The dealer plays god, of course. He uses his God-power to create happiness, to give peace of mind. His employees are efficient, capable, contented. He says: "We have never run an advertisement for an employee. When we need one, one comes to us; and he is always the right person."

Each of us can—and should—play god, all the time. Since we have God-power, why should we not let it be active in our life? Usually this God-power reveals itself to us in the form of ideas, and if we have the faith and courage to act on the divine intuition that comes to us, we reach the goals we aim for.

Newton Dillaway has said: "I defy anyone to show me a man who can work more quickly and efficiently under the guidance of a purely conscious method than under an intuitive one. . . . In any field of endeavor the one who does the best work is the one who is released, who has consented to be used by the universal power. And whether they know it or not is entirely beside the point. Most of them don't, and that is perhaps a good thing."

Right here we catch sight of the real secret of playing god: we do not *use* the God-power within us, we let it use us. The true source of any good work we do, any good results we accomplish, is intuitive guidance. When we let ourself be directed by this guidance, everything works together for good.

Perhaps it is just a matter of semantics, but to me it is unthinkable that I could ever "use God" or "use Truth" in any way. The God-power within me is not an obedient tool for me to use: it is a limitless supply of inspiration and ability for me to tap. And when I tap that power, I do not begin to shape it and manipulate it; I begin to make myself an instrument for its expression and achievement.

This is why I dare to believe Jesus' assurance that "You are gods"; this is why I can play god without any sense of arrogance or impropriety. And this is why you can remake your life by beginning to play god, every day and in every situation. If this were a matter of using God, or the God-power in you, you would surely fail. But it is not; it is wholly a matter of *being used,* of consenting to the flow and movement of God-power *through* you. If you are sure of this, you will surely succeed in achieving whatever goal you want to reach.

Listen for the Truth

There is an old folk saying to the effect that "If you know how to listen for the truth, you will never hear a lie." There are several ways we might interpret this. Perhaps the first that comes to mind has to do with the practice of "seeing the good in everything." In other words, if you know how to look for the good, you will see it, and you won't see faults, shortcomings, or evil.

But it seems to me that there is an even more significant interpretation of the instruction to "listen for the truth." Why is it that we frequently fail to demonstrate the good results we expect in our affairs? Isn't it because we don't really know, many times, how to "listen for the truth" . . . because we are accustomed to accepting the half-truth, the easy, inconsequential veneer of "positive thinking," rather than the hard reality of positive living?

The hard reality . . . yes, I think it is high time we say—firmly, but without any fear or trembling—that achieving successful results in Truth is no easier than any other approach to the good. For too long we have tried to insist (to ourselves, to others) that a metaphysical approach to life is somehow simpler and easier than an orthodox "religious" approach. But if we are quite honest with ourselves, we know this is not true.

Living in Truth certainly has many advantages. One of its greatest advantages is that it permits (even encourages) an honest appraisal of conditions and prospects. But knowing this, we still sometimes draw back a bit from the ultimate candor and honesty that is vital; we seem to prefer to try to "get by" on the words and phrases that come quickly to mind and fall glibly from the tongue. Because we are steeped in "the power of the word," we often stare so fixedly at words that we are blinded to the reality of Truth.

Consider, for example, several familiar situations in which we find ourselves.

One may say: "God wants me to be well, so if I *know* that I'm well, that's all there should be to it. But I'm still not really well!"

Listen for the truth: The mere intellectual knowing of any kind of truth has only an intellectual effect. Affirming that you are well usually will make you more cheerful and hopeful, mentally. But as long as you limit yourself to intellectual knowing, there can hardly be any physical healing.

There is something *you* have to do about any healing, something more than affirming that you are healed. You would not even be aware of a need for healing unless you were first aware of sickness, injury, or pain of some kind. So the first thing you have to do (and the most important thing) is an act of denial: you have to let go of whatever it is that has set up the need for healing.

Right here is where we run squarely up against the folly of trying to fool ourselves about the ease and simplicity of the Truth approach to living. Learning how to let go of what troubles you is probably the most diffi-

17

cult thing you will ever have to learn. Once learned, letting go *is* a simple, quick way to achieve results. But learning how can take a long time. Often the pieces seem to fall into place, finally, almost as if God were pushing us into the right answer. It is something no one else can do for you, or tell you exactly how to do; it is something you yourself must work out in your own thoughts and prayers. But it is so important . . . such a vital key to the whole process of demonstration and achievement . . . that it is worth devoting hours, days, weeks to. Don't be lulled into believing that you can affirm your way out of anything unpleasant, or into anything you desire. *Listen for the truth,* which is that until you learn how to "let go and let God," you are going to have to face recurring difficulties and lacks and problems. Begin to empty yourself completely to make room for God's power to work in you. Unless and until you know how to let go, your solutions will be only temporary.

Perhaps you have heard someone say (or perhaps you have said): "Love is the strongest force in the universe, so if I love everyone, all my problems should be solved. I don't dislike anyone; why doesn't everyone like me?"

Listen for the truth: Love is a force only if it is active. If love is merely a sentiment (no matter how commendable it may be), it has little power. An article in a newspaper said: "The only emotion that sustains men in prison is hatred; love is not a strong enough emotion." That is entirely true: as an emotion, love is no stronger than any other emotion, and it has only emotional effect. But if you have the determination and the know-how to take love out of the emotional category and make it an active force, what miracles it can work!

You say you don't dislike anyone, and probably you are being quite sincere. But how have you expressed your love for others? In these times (or in any times, for that matter) simply to be free of dislike isn't much better than to be filled with dislike. Not disliking anyone makes you neutral, and that means you don't accomplish anything on either side of the fence.

How do you express love, how make it an active force? Well, one way is (again) by denial: by putting away whatever is less-than-love. By not holding grudges . . . by deliberately and actively forgiving anyone against whom you have been holding thoughts that are condemning or deprecatory. "Real forgiveness is not a sentiment but a power." Do you have the courage to put that power to work in your affairs . . . all of them?

You say you don't dislike anyone. Do you *like* everyone? How many people know this? Do you ever go out of your way to tell someone how wonderful he is, or what a great job he is doing? Do you sometimes make it a point to praise someone who, you feel, doesn't really deserve it?

Someone has said, "If you tell people they are better than they really are, they will begin to think you are better than you really are." Of course! If you praise someone, he cannot help but see what insight and perception you have . . . and there is nothing dishonest on either side, because each of you is seeing through to the real person. Each of you is "listening for the truth."

Are you ever disappointed about the amount of prosperity you are demonstrating in your life? Do you ever think, for instance: "If I'm really a child of God, heir to all of His riches, why is it that I'm still in need so much of the time?"

Listen for the truth: "Seek first his kingdom and his righteousness, and all these things shall be yours as well." The operative word is *first*. And this does not mean a quick avowal of spirituality, followed by an avid impatience for material results. "We are not in Truth," says one writer, "for its perquisites but for itself. This means a certain indifference to the things . . . indifference as to how long they are in coming, as to whether they ever come—such is the paradoxical state of mind of one who knows that prosperity is inevitable."

Once we have honestly and genuinely begun to seek the kingdom first, and once we learn that this means we must also make it our ultimate search as well, we will be marvelously open to the rich sources of abundance that men call ideas.

For each facet of good that you want, you can probably find a facet of Truth that you have not adequately understood. And the Truth is too great, means too much to the world, to be dismissed or sloughed off through misunderstanding or misinterpretation. How many, I wonder, have given up in frustration and disappointment because they discovered that getting the right result was not just a matter of repeating positive words and phrases over and over!

You know what Truth means to you now. You know how much more you have a right to expect out of your life from now on. So don't risk the letdown that must inevitably follow any attempt to find an "easy" way out. Invest your life in the sure reality of Truth. *Listen for the truth.*

The Progress in Mistakes

I am God's perfect child. Therefore I don't make mistakes. Right?

Wrong.

I do make mistakes, just as you do.

But how is this possible? In a divinely ordered universe, how can a perfect child of God make mistakes? Isn't a mistake a contradiction in terms?

Not if I understand the true meaning of the word *mistake*. Webster says that a mistake is "a misunderstanding of the meaning or implication of something; a wrong action or statement proceeding from faulty judgment, inadequate knowledge, or inattention."

Yes, we are God's perfect children. But most of us don't express our perfection all the time, consistently. That's why life is full of opportunities for improvement, challenges to exciting, invigorating growth . . . and fun.

Most of the failures we encounter stem from misunderstanding—of God's laws, of human relations, of ourselves. Sometimes the only way God can catch our attention is through our mistakes. It would be foolish to think that God causes us to make mistakes; but it would be equally foolish to overlook the positive effects mistakes can have in our life.

Sometimes, if we're fortunate, and perceptive, we can look back and recognize the point in our affairs at which we received a startling bit of guidance . . . a clear-cut directive to move out in a new direction, or to make a certain decision. More frequently we can trace the thread of guidance back through the closely-woven fabric of our affairs to a point where we were brought up short by a seeming failure, or a seeming mistake that we have made.

Bernard Haldane, a brilliant writer and authority on personnel problems, says that it

24

is wrong to say that we "learn from our mistakes," and I think he's right. It isn't that our mistakes *teach* us . . . they *direct* us. A mistake is a road sign, perhaps a detour sign, a direction-finder.

There are too many historical instances of this to begin to enumerate. Take photography, for instance. Some of the very early experiments were made by a man named Niepce, who was later joined by a man named Daguerre. They were trying to develop a photographic plate, using silver salts on a silver plate, to produce an image. The experiments dragged on, apparently without success. Then one day Daguerre made a mistake.

He was experimenting with iodized silver plates. He exposed one as usual, on a bright, sunny day; then the clouds came over the sun, and Daguerre, who was already pretty discouraged, decided to call it a day. He packed up his plates and equipment and went home.

The next morning, when he took his equipment out, he took a casual look at the underexposed plate of the previous day. He was about to discard it, when he saw that the plate had taken on a clear likeness of the scene to which he had exposed it the day before. Checking, he found that the fumes of mercury, from an open container in his cupboard, had developed the image on the plate. This led him to the discovery of the solution that photographers now call the "hypo."

Daguerre gave his name to the process of making positive prints, called "daguerreotypes." At about the same time, a man named Talbot found out how to print images on white paper, like the negatives we know today, from which many positives could be printed.

Talbot called his invention the "calotype" process, and it too resulted from a mistake. His cat turned over an extract of nutgalls on some half-exposed papers coated with silver chloride. When Talbot saw what happened to the papers, he went on to develop his calotype process.

Sometimes it even seems that God has a "safety factor" in revealing His ideas to men. Someone has said that "no great discovery is ever left by nature to the efforts of just one man." Daguerre and Talbot were only two individuals who made significant discoveries in the same field almost simultaneously. Alexander Graham Bell is credited with inventing the telephone, in 1876; in the same year a less famous inventor, Elisha Grey, also invented a telephone, and he and Bell had never worked together in any way. The automobile engine was invented in America by Selden, in 1879; in the same year, Carl Benz invented the automobile engine in Germany. Thomas Edison invented the electric light bulb (after a spectacular series of "failures," "mistakes,") in New Jersey in 1880; J. W. Swan invented the electric light bulb in England in 1880.

A noted clergyman once said, gently poking fun at those who like to feel infallible, "Oh, we never make mistakes—but how the errors creep in!" Yet mistakes would be impossible in a properly-ordered, divinely-guided universe . . . unless there were some evidence that mistakes have a place in the divine order of things.

I think they *do* have a place. (How discouraging it would be to believe that our mistakes are just pointless, dumb stumbling!) I believe that a mistake is a nudge from God . . . a friendly, helpful nudge in the right

27

direction. So when I make a mistake, I know it's time to pay closer attention. I don't like to be nudged, particularly, but if that is the only way God can get my attention . . .

What Will You Have?

Only a most unperceptive person could fail to be aware of today's changing social mores and patterns of behavior. Of course change in attitudes and actions is a normal part of the growth and development of mankind, but sometimes change seems to come more quickly, more impressively, than at other times. One such period of rapid changes was that following World War I, the era that came to be known as the "jazz age." However, many sociologists, educators, and spiritual leaders feel that the changes in our own day are even more revolutionary in nature than those of the 1920s.

29

Traditionally, organized religion has seemed to range itself against change . . . and this is not difficult to understand. When we think of man's spiritual nature and his spiritual quest, we think of the "eternal verities," the changeless nature of God, the enduring truth of God. A special kind of understanding is called for if we are to stand firm in our faith, and at the same time welcome the changes in contemporary thought and behavior that are good for mankind. This understanding is the rare gift that we are given when we think through the challenges of everyday living with a steadfast faith that Truth does not change, that God's plan for the human race is never altered . . . that "underneath are the everlasting arms" of God, regardless of the upheavals and confusions on the surface of modern life.

It is fashionable to speak of "the new morality," usually with approval or with criticism. If we take time to think it through, however, we come to realize that there is nothing really "new" about most of the widely-accepted moral views of today. What *is* new is the growing acceptance, by spiritually minded persons, of a more realistic, constructive attitude toward many aspects of morality long considered to be off limits to "good people."

Many of us would like to be able to set down, in a few well-chosen words, a simple, straightforward code of conduct that would be both moral and contemporary. Of course it *is* possible to be both moral and contemporary . . . but it is not easy to make rules to cover such conduct. About all we can do is try to formulate a few statements that will guide us in meeting the challenges of behavior and conduct that face us day by day.

First of all, we must determine what it is that we believe about ourself and our relationships with other people. We can surely agree, then, on this basic statement: Every individual is entitled to evaluate himself, and to be evaluated by others, as a child of God, with all the infinite potential that this implies.

We can also agree on a corollary: It is the responsibility of every child of God to express as much of his infinite potential as he possibly can. If I can express all of my potential, then I do the "greater things" that Jesus promised each of us might do; if, like most of us, I work *toward* this supreme goal, I express a

31

little more of my potential from day to day.

It is an axiom of living that as we strive toward any goal, we have choices to make. This is part of the striving. None of us is fortunate enough to see the road ahead laid out straight and undeviating . . . "smooth sailing" to the ultimate harbor. And it is in the making of choices and decisions that we earn the right to be called followers after Christ.

One of the thorny points of theology and religious philosophy has always been the matter of man's freedom of will. On the one hand we are confronted with the traditional, highly orthodox belief that man's life is predetermined and governed by God . . . that man comes into the world with his life's work somehow laid out for him, his destiny fixed, and that, strive as he will, he cannot really change his destiny. No thinking man today quite believes this.

On the other hand we have the belief that man is the supreme arbiter of his destiny; that whatever happens, he is the supreme master of his fate, and he can change any condition in his life simply by thinking positively about the possibility of a better condition. No thinking man quite believes this, either, though we would *like* to believe it implicitly; nothing is more heartening to one who is down-and-out than the notion that all of his unpleasant circumstances can be altered for the better simply by changing his thoughts for the better.

India's great Nehru once expressed himself on these matters in words that strike to the heart of it. He said: "There is no natural conflict or inconsistency between free will and determinism. Life is both. Life is like a game of cards. The hand that is dealt you represents determinism. The way you play it is free will. So I think I have perhaps learned that it is better to make the most of what you are than to rue yourself into exhaustion because you are not someone else."

These are not "religious" words, but they mean a great deal to the man or woman trying to find a solution to the problems of modern life.

It has often been charged that metaphysical thinking and metaphysical movements preach a "sweetness and light" approach to life that is as impractical as it is pleasant. And if we try to make ourself, or others, believe that all of our problems can be solved mentally, or by the simple process of affirming positive words, we are going to be (sooner or later) sadly disappointed at the results.

If we as Christians have a fault (and it is just possible that we *do* have, even the best of us!) it is our too-eager grasping at the forms and words of Truth. Once we accept the fact that words and thoughts have power, we are all too prone to rely entirely on this power, to the exclusion of the conscious *effort* that we must exercise to activate the power.

One of Emerson's most familiar quotations is: "What will you have? quoth God; pay for it and take it." It is the sort of quotation that grips the imagination . . . but all too often, it summons up visions of dire consequences. It is usually accepted as a warning, a notice served on mankind that everything desired has its price—usually a price too dear to pay.

Actually the only warning inherent in these words is this: Be sure that you know what the price is, and be sure that the price is not exorbitant.

"Pay for it and take it." There could be no more wonderful promise of good! What the promise implies is that any good desire (or any bad desire, for that matter) can be achieved if one is willing to pay the price. Turned around, the promise is that there is no desire beyond achievement; all that is required is a willingness, and the ability, to pay for what is wanted.

It is almost inevitable that our growth and development should at times seem to conflict with the happiness and progress of others we meet. But note the word *seem*, because any such conflict is only apparent. What happens is that our belief as to what is right and good is not in harmony with someone else's belief. We may be right, or he may be right . . . but one of us *is* right; and if the one who is right allows himself to be deflected for any reason, he fails in his responsibility to himself as a child of God.

No one could possibly tell you in advance just what to do in every specific situation that you will meet in your life. Even when a confusing situation arises, it would be difficult for anyone else to advise you on its outcome. Knowing what is right for you—knowing how to find the right answer in a given set of circumstances—is something that must grow within you, developing surely and steadily as you cultivate your own God-given awareness of the truth about yourself.

Because we love those around us, we sometimes impede their growth and development, and are false to ourself, by choosing a certain course through fear of "hurting" others. It is hardly possible to go through life without hurting others, if by this we mean the outward response to human situations. And if we make all our judgments, base all our choices, on the theory that we must never do anything to disappoint or disagree with those who love us, we will really hurt them more, in the long run, than if we make true judgments and choices based on our inner knowledge of the truth.

Particularly in the sensitive area of human relations, we must be entirely true to our inner self. It is only when we are completely sure of our own right answer, and act on that sureness, that we truly fulfill our responsibility to ourself and to others about us.

In human relations, we sometimes tend to feel that a proper balance, a harmonious relationship with someone else is unattainable. But nothing is unattainable if we are willing to pay the price, and almost daily we are asked to make decisions regarding the price of some relationship we want (or think we want.) Often the price is relatively low: if we want to resolve some minor conflict with an acquaintance, we have only to pay the price of making the first move toward friendship. Again, the price may be quite high, as in the case of dissolving some relationship of long standing.

The situations change, and the price may be low or high. But always the important point is our awareness of the price, and our willingness to take an honest look at the price.

In the great majority of situations we are faced with day by day, the decisions are virtually automatic, and that is good. Deciding whether the price would be exorbitant or fair is something we do almost without thinking. If I am hungry, I do not make a long, solemn appraisal of the desirability of eating; I sit down and eat. There are too many minute-by-minute decisions in human life for us to devote conscious thought to each one. We do not decide to take a breath; we just breathe in and out. In these routine matters, our subconscious takes over and makes decisions with computer-like efficiency, and we are freed to take careful, conscious thought for the major decisions.

Right here, however, is where we *can* get into trouble. Because we are so used to taking action without conscious thought, we may do so to the exclusion of decision-making that is vital. If I am hungry, I sit down and eat. But what if I am overweight? If I still sit down and eat, without thinking about my weight problem, I have abdicated my decision-making authority. I have given no thought to the price involved. Subconsciously I realize that I am overeating, and that this is going to affect my health and well-being; but I take no conscious notice of this. In effect, I pay the price without evaluating my purchase.

So the essential factor is (as always) our awareness of the price, and our conscious determination that the price is in line. In moral and ethical matters, we can (and should) make a basic evaluation and hold to it: at some point in life, we evaluate the course we set for ourself and decide that this is what we want our life to mean; this is what we want to accomplish in life, and the price required (in human relationships and every-

38

thing else) is worth what we want to achieve.

Only disaster can result if we go through life (or even a part of life) recklessly paying for what we want without knowing whether or not the price is right. Only good can come if we consciously evaluate the important situations that come up, decide on the price we believe is right, and resolutely pay that price for the good we want.

Insisting on having what we want, regardless of the price, is an invitation to trouble. By the same token, refusing to pay the price once we have set a course is a form of betrayal of self and principle that can only produce bad results.

In short, the importance of the quotation is in its positive aspect, rather than in the negative. It is not that we should be constantly apprehensive because "everything has its price"; rather, we should be constantly thankful and expectant because there is nothing we cannot have by paying the price. This is the key to activating our thoughts and words. The price for what we want may be a stronger, deeper faith; it may be some form of concrete action. What matters is that there *is* a price that will purchase the good we want—not money, but thoughts, words, deeds.

There are those (and I am among them) who believe that many of today's young people are discovering and practicing a more realistic, sensible, decent standard of moral conduct than men have known for centuries. In the face of careless criticism of youth at loose ends, it is nevertheless becoming more and more apparent to those who take the trouble to examine contemporary behavior that in many cases, today's young men and women are setting standards for themselves that are often far higher than those we set a generation or two ago. The best of them, for instance, are putting sex in its proper context . . . not glorifying it or debasing it, but seeing it as a natural, wonderful facet of living. No, the new generation is not perfect; it may even have as many imperfections as my generation had . . . but it seems to me that among some of its leaders, it is exhibiting a sense of responsibility and maturity found in few generations before it. (A recent article in a popular magazine, by a respected sociologist, said: "Actually, the family may be moving into the Golden Age. . . . Marriage—firmly and willfully welded, centered on creative parenthood—may become the future's most stable institution.")

A new morality? No, rather a new and more perceptive approach to morality itself (there is no such thing as "old" or "new" morality, because morality is an absolute). If we are willing, as open-minded followers after Truth, to rethink our standards of conduct and behavior, we will come to realize that the old rules still apply after all: Each of us has a responsibility to others, and to himself—the responsibility of expressing his own potential, and making it possible for others to express their potential. And we will know, too, that we fulfill that responsibility only when we act firmly and lovingly, in every human relationship, true to the best that we know.

* * *

On one of the walls of my office there is a poster, given to me by one of my co-workers. It bears these words, attributed to Frederick S. Perls:

"I do my thing and you do your thing.

I am not in this world to live up to your expectations, and you are not in this world to live up to mine.

You are you, and I am I ... and if by

41

chance we find each other, *it's beautiful!*"

Of all the catch phrases originating with the "now" generation, that may be the truest and most apt of all: "Do your own thing." It is not an apology for dropping out; it is a statement of personal integrity. It is also a worthy goal to work toward.

It is not just a matter of not interfering with someone else's way of life. That is certainly right, and commendable. But even more important is having the self-knowledge, and the courage, to pursue one's own way of life, without worrying about what others say or think.

To have "the courage of your convictions," you must have convictions. To do your own thing, you must have something positive to do. It is not a matter of refusing to participate; it is a matter of choosing a course and sticking to it. It calls for thinking things through, considering the alternatives, and then making a firm decision.

Having done this, I can (and must) go ahead, regardless of what "they" think. Certainly I want others to like me and approve of me, but that is not the greatest thing to be desired. If I can win others' approval, wonderful! . . . but only if I can do it without making others' expectations my criterion. My purpose in life is not to live up to the expectations of anyone else, and by the same token I cannot expect others to seek my approval first.

We would surely agree that the greatest satisfactions we find in life are in the relationships we have with our fellowmen. You and I may never know a celebrity well enough to call him by his first name, but we may find equal (or greater) enjoyment in talking across the fence with a neighbor.

Yes, human relationships are the source of most of the real beauty we know in living. And sooner or later we learn that any relationship with another has something in common with the cactus: we derive full pleasure from it only so long as we are content to accept it as it is, without trying to grasp and mold it.

The beauty of the cactus is a blessing to be savored, not grasped and hugged to oneself. So it is with a friendship, or a marriage, or any other human relationship.

The cactus really has just a single purpose: to live and grow, to express the life form inherent within it. The beauty of its bloom is a happy by-product. Men may enjoy that beauty, but only by not trying to clasp it. The sharp spines of the cactus plant are there to discourage those (men or animals) who would uproot or consume it. To grasp the cactus carelessly would be a painful mistake. It is possible to transplant a cactus, but only with care and skill.

Just so it is with our human relationships: It is always a mistake (often a painful mistake) to carelessly try to hug to oneself, for one's own reasons, the radiating love and beauty in another person's nature. When we love someone, we can give that love roots in our own life and affairs—but only by exercising unselfish care and skill in the doing. A careless, blind grasping and pulling can only bring pain, and may destroy the relationship entirely.

We should not forget, either, that doing my own thing doesn't necessarily separate me from anyone else. Why should I feel that my convictions, my life style, are automatically different from those of other men and women of good will? In fact, my determination to do my own thing should make me even more aware of (and receptive to) the ideas and strivings of others . . . and certainly readier to approve *your* determination to do *your* own thing.

The slow but steady process of creating a better world calls for the concerted efforts of all who believe in themselves strongly enough to do their own thing. "And if by chance we find each other, it's beautiful!" But more often than not, it will not be by chance, but as part of God's grand design.

The Powerful Principle of Prosperity

You can share the wealth of God. An abundance of all good things can be yours. Prosperity, spiritual and material prosperity, is yours for the taking. All that is required is your faithful application of God's law of abundance.

How do we know that God's law of abundance works? How do we know that it is an active principle that we can lay hold of and use, and not merely a pleasant happenstance?

We know because we experience the action of God's law. Or perhaps we see its action, clear and unmistakable, in the affairs of another. This knowledge, this certainty, is not

47

something rare, limited to a few. It is a matter of universal realization, among men of every nation and creed. For those who have seen or experienced the powerful principle of prosperity at work, there is no doubt that it *does* work.

In 1632 Galileo Galilei published a now-famous treatise giving support to the theory that the earth revolves around the sun. This was contrary to the ecclesiastical beliefs of his day, and he was called before the Inquisition and ordered to recant. This he finally agreed to do, perhaps realizing the futility of trying to force a new idea upon authorities who had set their minds against the truth.

Before a great assemblage, Galileo knelt and publicly renounced his belief in the system of the universe as we now believe it to be constituted, including the earth's movement around the sun. But according to legend, he was heard to whisper, as he arose from his knees, "Nevertheless it does move."

Fact or fiction, the words attributed to Galileo are a symbolic expression of the Truth that cannot be denied, the reality that cannot be doubted by those who have experienced it. "Nevertheless it does move," Galileo is said to have murmured, insisting against powerful opposition that the earth does revolve around the sun, and is not the stationary center of the universe. "Nevertheless it works!" men of all ages have said, in effect, when confronted with doubt or disparagement of God's law.

Once we have had personal knowledge of the working of the law of abundance, we marvel that we ever should have doubted. It seems incredible that what we know to be the perfect outworking of God's plans should be considered as coincidence, luck, or accident.

I have proved God's law of abundance in my own affairs; I have applied His great principles of prosperity to attain both material and spiritual abundance. I have known the working of His laws; I know it now, every day. Sometimes He works in ordered, expected ways to manifest that which I need or desire; sometimes

"God moves in a mysterious way
His wonders to perform."

Though I am not wealthy, I have used the prospering principles of Truth to attain an abundance of the material blessings that make life pleasant. Wouldn't I like to be wealthy? Perhaps; although money is not an obsession

49

with me, I do not deny that I would be glad to have more of it. But you see, I lay no claim to making *perfect* use of God's law; I merely state that I have used it and am using it as well as my present spiritual development permits. Because I have experienced God's abundant good in some measure, I am confident that a greater, as yet unimagined measure is still to be experienced.

The largest diamond yet discovered, the Cullinan, weighed 3,025 carats (about a pound and a half)—yet it is believed to be only part of a larger, still undiscovered stone. The belief in the existence of an even greater diamond does not dim the brilliance of presently known stones. Nor does our expectation of a more effective application of God's law of abundance dim our joy in the results already attained through using the law as best we could.

Most of my own demonstrations of prosperity have been unspectacular, at least to others. But there are enough spectacular demonstrations on record (well-documented record, mind you) to satisfy the skeptical.

"People who say they don't believe in miracles should see us now," said a California housewife. Her husband had started a plumbing contracting business with little capital. With teen-age children in high school, the mother had written to Unity for prayers. She received assurance of Silent Unity's prayers, and affirmations to use.

"Knowing your prayers were with us, we (all four of us) prayed together and absolutely left everything to God," she said later. "We have what we need and as much as we can assimilate. We find ourselves praying now that we may be big enough to receive all the good God has for us. My husband has all the work he can handle and more to come, our bills are being paid up fast, and our daily needs have been more than supplied."

If what is desired is evidence of God's instant help in emergency, consider this testimony of an Iowa woman:

"We have just moved to a new town where I knew no one. Several weeks ago my husband went out of town on business for the day, and phoned later to say that he would have to be gone for several days. After I hung up the receiver, I found to my dismay that I had only five dollars in the house, few groceries, no way of obtaining more money, and no way

51

to contact my husband. Besides, I had faithfully promised to pay six dollars to a man the following morning.

"That evening before going to bed I happened to think of the story of Jesus' experience with the two fishes and the loaves of bread. I sat and thought, and I wondered how God could possibly multiply my five dollars to meet our needs for the next few days. I must admit that I had a heavy heart—but I prayed before I went to sleep that somehow help would come.

"Just as I was dropping off to sleep the doorbell rang. When I answered it, I found a man from a distant town whom I did not know, but who said he owed my husband $50. He insisted that I take the money and give him a receipt, which I did.

"When I returned to bed I suddenly realized that within a few hours God had multiplied my original five dollars by ten—giving me more than enough to see me through."

Of course all these things are theory, and no more, as far as you are concerned—until you prove the prospering principle in your own life.

We think of wealth as an abundance of

"worldly goods." Sometimes we use those words disparagingly, as though anything worldly were somehow undesirable. In truth, however, it is in the world of our daily affairs that we grow and progress, spiritually as well as materially; and we have a right to an abundance of the good that is in and of the world.

"Worldly goods" are the good things that God has placed in His world for us; so we claim them as we claim all the blessings of God, material and spiritual—through our firm faith that God intends us to have them abundantly.

We can learn to prove the promises of God consistently, day by day. Our first demonstrations are likely to seem miraculous, but as our prosperity continues to be manifested, regularly and surely, we shall come to see it for what it is: our rightful share of the wealth of God.

Let's Get Into the Act

Surely nobody objects to the idea of giving thanks. No one has to make a case for thanksgiving. It would call for real perversity of character to claim that gratitude is out of place. All of us, it would seem, are in favor of gratitude and thanksgiving . . . but sometimes we tend to accept the notion that someone else should be expressing these virtues.

Jimmy Durante has a famous punch line which he has used in his characteristic fashion for many years: "Everybody wants to get into the act!" When it comes to putting principles to work, everybody should get into the act . . . should replace talk with action,

55

wishing with doing, nodding agreement with positive performance.

We can think of thanksgiving as any one of a variety of "acts," each of which (or all of which) can have deep significance in our day-by-day growth and progress.

On the most elementary level, of course, thanksgiving is simply an *act of courtesy*. But the fact that this is elementary should not cause us to discount its importance. Courtesy, in the words of a favorite cliché, provides the oil that lubricates the machinery of everyday living. The many, many "thank yous" we may hear in the course of any day are actually quite important to the pleasure we get out of that day.

Of course a sincere "thank you" is better than a mechanical rejoinder . . . but even the mechanical variety is better than none. In fact, there is something to be said for the civilized approach to daily affairs that can make "thank you" automatic, something to be said without thinking. Doesn't it surprise you when (infrequently) a salesperson or someone else neglects to say "thank you" in the course of a simple transaction? And don't you wonder how anyone can go through a day (or even a single encounter with another human being) without just naturally using the routine words of appreciation?

On what is perhaps the next higher level, gratitude is an *act of appreciation*. This includes such to-be-expected expressions of thanksgiving as letting someone know that you appreciate what he has done, or what he is. It may also include such things as being aware of one's good ... and letting that awareness show.

Many of us (probably most of us) are not as emotional as we could be (should be). We are too much accustomed to expressing ourselves on an intellectual, or reasoning, level. Feeling carried to the extreme of an "ism"—emotionalism—involves certain risks: of being misunderstood, of giving the wrong impression, and so on. But the rigid kind of self-control that precludes any show of feeling, that hides all emotion behind a mask of logic and intellect, has built-in risks that are even greater: the risk of loneliness, the risk of suspicion, the risk of frustration. As in all of living, a balance is needed. But if an exact balance cannot be struck, it is probably better to let the scales be weighted a bit on the side

of feeling and emotion. It is better to express
our thanksgiving and appreciation by *showing*
how much we are aware of our good. Honest
emotion is seldom misunderstood in the long
run.

Being thankful can also be an *act of involvement.* The fact that we love someone, or
some thing—an institution, perhaps—doesn't
mean that we automatically approve of that
person, or thing, in every respect. Often we
have to make our lack of approval plain
(without rancor) simply because we *do* love.

The easiest way to love anyone or anything
is uncritically. Lovers know what a tempta-
tion it can be to close their eyes to faults and
shortcomings . . . and to an extent, this is
wise. We do not enter into any kind of love
with a desire to find fault, and as far as
possible we overlook the little faults even
when we find them. But if something appears
that is clearly wrong, in our sight, and we
refuse to see it or try to correct it, we really
betray the object of our love.

This is particularly true with regard to
institutions, organizations, even nations.
Refusing to admit that there are shortcomings, or on the other hand, dropping out

58

because we see faults, are unrealistic and uncourageous acts. "Love it or leave it" is a craven slogan; "Love it and improve it" is the positive approach. If we are thankful for blessings, love, or good we have received from someone or some group, we should make our appreciation an act of involvement . . . have the courage and determination to work actively for the growth and improvement of what we love.

On the highest level, we can think of thanksgiving as an *act of faith*. All the teachers we respect assure us that by expressing our gratitude in advance we actually open the way for the desired good to manifest itself in our life. One of Charles Fillmore's favorite teachings was that "true thanksgiving may be likened to rain falling upon ready soil, refreshing it and increasing its productiveness." He said, "Praise and thanksgiving impart the quickening spiritual power that produces growth and increase in all things."

As is the case with most of the principles of Truth, you need not accept this on anyone else's say-so; you can easily prove it. In fact, this may be one of the simplest of all principles to prove, because you have nothing to do except be grateful. Even if the thought of saying "thank you" in advance is new to you, and seems a trifle strange, you can try it merely in the sense of playing a role: act as though you are thankful for something you are praying for, and watch the results.

Gardner Hunting expressed it well, when he recalled William James' suggestion that instead of laughing because we are happy, "we are happy because we laugh; sad because we weep, brave because we face our danger; we love because we serve." All this is profoundly true, Hunting said, adding: "It occurs to me that, instead of giving because we are thankful, it may be that we grow thankful because we give. . . . Prosperity, yes, surprising prosperity; but thankfulness—that seems to be the very *cause* of blessings, for which I thank Him in advance."

Thanksgiving . . . act of courtesy, act of appreciation, act of involvement, act of faith. Why shouldn't we all get into the act?

What Should I Say to God?

A few years ago, in the course of my editorial work, I received two letters from two different young people. The first was from a girl named Evelyn, who wanted advice on how to pray.

"I've just begun to realize that I don't know how to pray in the true sense of the word," she writes. "When I go to church on Sunday I pray, but I still don't feel that I understand what I should say to God."

In answering Evelyn's letter, I pointed out, first of all that if you want to pray, there are not many mistakes you *can* make, because wanting to pray is the most important part of praying. One mistake that can keep you from getting the most out of prayer, however, is to regard it as complicated or mysterious or difficult.

Prayer means many things to many persons. In the minds of some, solemn rituals and ceremonies are part of prayer. We who make simple prayer part of our lives can also respect and participate in the language and rites of formal worship. But we feel, through our own experience with simple prayer, that a quiet talk with God is the finest kind of refreshing, uplifting interlude in today's busy living.

If you feel that you must have certain conditions and surroundings before you pray, you are sometimes unable to go to God when you most need to talk with Him. That is why the first step in learning how to pray is to understand that prayer is, simply and wonderfully, talking with God.

Perhaps *talking* is not the most accurate word to use, for often nothing is said aloud. A better word might be *communing*—a word that does not deserve the air of awesome mystery it often seems to have. Communing might be defined as "thinking together." The best of friends are those we commune with;

they are ones who are so close to us that we can spend much time with them without saying more than a few words aloud. Words are not always necessary among good friends; we learn to share one another's thoughts and emotions, and we feel an intangible but very real bond even in the midst of a noisy crowd.

So it is—or can be—in our relationship with God. In fact, the togetherness can be even more real, because God is closer to us than any friend; He is within us. The thoughts that we think come from God originally, so it is just a matter of re-attuning our minds with His mind. Then we are thinking together with God—and this is the most effective kind of prayer.

Of course, getting in tune with God's way of thinking is not something that we can do automatically, as we would switch on an electric light. We cannot commune with God if some of our thoughts are miles away—on the bills, or the weather, or anything of the sort. We have to be genuinely interested in God's ideas if we expect to pray effectively.

Such a requirement is not unreasonable, is it? If you had occasion to ask a banker to lend you a sum of money and kept your appointment with him disinterestedly, he probably would decide against making the loan. If, while the banker told you the conditions under which you would be permitted to borrow the needed money, you kept staring out the window, watching passers-by on the sidewalk, the banker might be expected to feel that you were not really interested in securing the money.

God has a right to expect as much courtesy and interested attention as we would give to any good friend in conversation. The only way to center our thoughts on God is to approach Him in a mood that is in keeping with His nature: an attitude of reverence and worship. Here again, it is wise to remember that worship does not necessarily mean kneeling in a church, or going through any similar ritual. Worship *may* be formal; most of us find it helpful and inspiring to worship God publicly, solemnly, and with ceremony at regular intervals. But such worship is an extra, or an added dividend of good. The basic good is the good we come to know through informal, private worship. God is never unapproachable or remote. We can go to Him at any time, in any surroundings, regardless of companions or conditions.

Silence is an essential part of prayer; but the silence must be within us, not necessarily around us. Practice will make possible a genuine inner silence that we can achieve whenever we need to commune with God.

"What should I say to God?" We know that it is not necessary to say anything aloud, unless we particularly want to speak. Sometimes it is helpful to speak; it helps us to realize the presence of God. If you feel that you can more surely and reverently approach God by speaking, then you should speak. Even so, you need not speak loudly; a whisper, or even forming the words in your mind, will do as well.

What you should say is whatever seems most helpful under the circumstances. Different situations may call for different expressions. The best way to find out what words you want to use in approaching God is to experiment. Throughout the pages of Truth books and magazines you can find different affirmations—sentences or phrases that have helped others to recognize God's presence. Repeat—aloud or silently—one of these affirmations when you go to God. Or use any sentence, phrase, or word that comes to your mind; if you truly want to approach Him, God will come more than halfway to meet you. He will put the right thought into your mind.

I remember one of Gardner Hunting's articles that told of a man who, when he wanted to bring his thoughts into harmony with God's thinking, said simply, "Now, Lord." Emmet Fox said that a favorite affirmation of his was "God is with me." Even the word *God* is a powerful thought in itself.

At any rate, you will find that it is easy to contact God. He is so close—"closer . . . than breathing, and nearer than hands and feet." He is not an awesome, remote deity with whom you must make a formal appointment; He is within you, always immediately available when you need Him.

Once you have learned to recognize His presence, once you know (and it is so easy, so simple to know!) how to approach Him, you are praying. But then, you may ask again, "What should I say?" And again, the answer is: "You can say a great deal or very little. You can bring your most complicated problems, your most cherished ideals and discuss

66

them with Him; or you can just relax in His presence, with the sure knowledge that He is solving your problems, adjusting all your affairs, bringing about what you most want to achieve and be."

Should you pray about specific things? You may if you want to; many persons do, and their prayers are answered. But you are sure to find, as you gain experience in praying, that the wisest prayer is the prayer that lets God make your decisions and choices.

We can pray for the friendship of one certain person, bearing in mind always that God's plans for us include the friendship of all around us and brotherhood that is wide enough to encircle the whole world. We can ask in prayer for the successful outcome of a test or examination, knowing that God's infinite wisdom is ours to use in all that we undertake—that He works with us to bring about good results in all that we study, profitable use of all that we learn.

God is interested in us; He wants us to share with Him every condition, situation, and association affecting our lives. No seeming trouble is too small to bring to Him for adjustment; no dream is too remote, no ideal too high to entrust to Him. No good thing that we want to undertake is farfetched in God's sight. He knows the unlimited power that is within us, even though we may never have demonstrated our talents and abilities.

We should place every detail of our living in God's keeping. We should never think of anyone or anything in a negative, critical way. We should consider not what is wrong but what is right. We should not see any discouraging or inharmonious situation as it appears to be, but as it will be when God adjusts it. We should see good developing out of every circumstance, even though we are not able to see exactly how the development will take place.

I say this not in a manner of preaching or teaching; I say it simply by way of relating what prayer has meant to me. I have prayed in this way many times, in many situations. This simple way of praying—this thinking together with God, seeing the good and letting Him work it out as He sees fit—has helped me in business, in relationships with others, in planning my affairs. There is nothing exclusive, nothing mysterious, nothing complicated about it.

"What should I say to God?" Say what

comes naturally; do not wait for special words to come. Do not strive for perfect sentences, polished phrases. Go to God as you would go to any good friend; share your thoughts with Him, and He will share His ideas with you. And almost before you know it, you will come to realize that all your thoughts, all your actions are part of prayer.

There is no more heartening thing to know. It is something to hold in your mind, something you will never lose.

It will make all the hours of your life richer and fuller.

How to Make It Work for You

Within a day or so after I had answered Evelyn's letter, I received a letter from another young woman, Lenore. She made a point about some of our articles and books that deserved a candid answer, and I tried to give it to her.

"In so many of your articles you say that you can be anything, do anything you want, if you really want to," Lenore wrote, "I cannot understand this, because I am handicapped with a heart condition that has been present for fourteen years."

The articles and books that say "you can be anything, do anything you want," are not made up of glib, empty promises. You *can* be anything; you *can* do anything. What is the catch? There is no catch. There is an *if,* of course; otherwise, the promise would be meaningless. What is the *if?* "If you really want to." If you *really* want to—want to enough to act your desire, to give substance to your wanting.

There are two steps in overcoming any undesirable condition: denying the reality of the seeming evil, and letting in the reality of the good. Lenore wants to let the good in; she wants to believe—but she hampers herself by giving equal room in her mind to doubt. "I am handicapped," she says. This is a commonplace statement for one with her health condition, and she probably makes the statement almost automatically, without thought of the harm it causes. But when she says "I am handicapped," she lends reality to the condition she wants to overcome.

No one should ever say, aloud or to himself, "I am handicapped." There are no handicaps in God's sight. No circumstance is a handicap if it leads one to express God. And many seemingly unpleasant circumstances do just that: they lead one to a fuller expression of the Christ within.

Lenore has read many stories, true stories, about persons who have overcome handicaps. We will not tell her any such stories now. The purpose of such stories is not, in any case, to provide specific instruction in how to overcome one's particular "handicap," but to offer proof that overcoming is possible. Lenore has seen that proof. She believes. "I am thrilled when I read your stories of how people overcome their handicaps," she says, "but it doesn't work for me."

It works. It works for others, and it works for you. It always works. It is no dazzling miracle that God works to effect a change in a specific situation; it is a law, an everlasting, ever-working law of God. If it works in one case, it will work in every case. Lenore does not doubt that it works in some cases; she has read of these cases and has been thrilled by the stories. So she is, at least, halfway toward her own overcoming. She has faith that God's healing power works "sometimes." All she needs to do now is to believe that God is consistent, that He is impartial, that His will is *always* good. This is not so hard to believe, is it?

You see, it is not really necessary that Lenore see someone else overcome the undesirable condition that she herself has. Perhaps no one else with exactly the same handicap has overcome it; perhaps Lenore can pioneer in spiritual overcoming. We know (and so does Lenore) that so-called handicaps often open doors to unimagined accomplishments. Someone has said, "Those who have normal health and beauty often do not feel called upon to excel in any other way, and often fail to realize the wonder of the gifts they possess; but often those who are physically handicapped are more inclined to turn within and discover the Christ power that gives them greater stamina and courage."

"The doctors do not allow me to work, and they forbid me to go out where there are any people," Lenore goes on. Having sought the advice of doctors, one should not disregard the advice that is given; but this is not to say that one should accept a doctor's advice as the final verdict in any case. Few doctors would want their patients to accept such advice as the "last word." It is possible (and most desirable) to begin to work toward God's perfect healing even while obeying a doctor's orders. Every good physician would be delighted to know that his patients are thinking and praying their way to health—and most doctors acknowledge that *wanting* to be healthy in both mind and body, is a vital step in physical healing.

"I feel as if I have no purpose in life," Lenore says. She has also said, "I have the gift of music in me, but what good does it do, as I cannot use it?" Of course, Lenore has a purpose in life; of course, she is needed in God's perfect plan. If she feels that she has the gift of music, there is some way in which she can put this gift to use to give purpose to her life. And she can begin to make use of her gift right now, regardless of her physical condition.

In one of his letters to the Corinthians, Paul says:

"There are varieties of gifts, but the same Spirit; and there are varieties of service, but the same Lord; and there are varieties of working, but it is the same God who inspires them all in every one."

And a little later, he adds, "But all these effects are produced by one and the same Spirit, apportioning them severally to each individual as he pleases."

If Lenore recognizes that she has God's gift of music in her, then she can use this gift in some good way. There are many persons who have the gift of music, but are not musicians. Some of those with the most sincere dedication to music play no instruments, sing no songs; their dedication is a humble and an unselfish thing, a deep appreciation of the music created and interpreted by others. One need not be a creator to make use of one's God-given talents. Of equal value, in God's great scheme, is he who appreciates and enjoys what another creates. "To have great poets, there must be great audiences too," Walt Whitman said. Lenore may well paraphrase these words in connection with her gift of music. If she learns to be a great and perceptive listener now, she will be using and developing God's gift—and perhaps, at the same time, preparing herself for creative expression at some later time.

Lenore's greatest problem, perhaps, is that she is too open-minded. We generally think of an open mind as good, and so it is; but we must make certain that our minds are open only to the good, and not to anything and everything that we see or hear or experience. Lenore reads the many fine stories about those who have overcome handicaps, and she is thrilled; but she weighs her faith against her doubts, her past experiences, and comes to the fearful conclusion, "It doesn't work for me."

We should never leave our minds open to the negative. Charles Fillmore, writing about Peter's unfortunate attempt to walk on the water ("He was afraid, and beginning to sink, he cried out, 'Lord, save me' "), says of him: "He saw too much wetness in the water. He saw the negative side of the proposition, and it weakened his demonstration. If you want to demonstrate, never consider the negative side."

Lenore's fine letter closes with the words, "I would appreciate any advice you can give me." She could have no better advice than that of Mr. Fillmore: "If you want to demonstrate, never consider the negative side." She has not yielded to unbelief, she has not said flatly, "I'll never accomplish anything, because of my heart condition." But she has weakened her faith simply by admitting that the possibility of failure exists. In her sincere desire to think things through in her own mind, she has seen "too much wetness in the water." She has been thinking in several different directions, instead of being single-minded.

Just three sentences in Lenore's letter illustrate how her tolerance of the negative has weakened her ability to believe. "They say that sickness comes to a person because he has sinned. That I do not understand. I have lived a good life."

It is true that sickness may be the result of sin. However, the word *sin* has a wider meaning than we commonly attribute to it. If Lenore is thinking that sickness always comes as a result of doing something immoral, illegal, or evil, she is mistaken. Lenore knows in her heart that she has not sinned in that sense of the word—so she can be sure that her physical disability is not the punishment of God. God is good; God does not punish anyone, ever. To sin is to miss the mark, to fail to measure up to the good in every detail—and, thus, sin contains its own consequences.

To be truly good means more than to be morally good, although this is part of it. Being good means not worrying, not becoming angry, never feeling dejected, depressed, or that life is unjust.

No, Lenore's sickness is not a punishment for sin; it is not a punishment at all. There is some other reason—a reason based on some law that she ignored or trespassed, perhaps unknowingly. The very feeling that she cannot overcome her handicap and that she has no purpose in life is a "sin," in the true sense, and undoubtedly has some part in keeping her down.

Prayer will help Lenore now, more than anything else, to get the right view of herself, of God, and of life. Prayer can awaken in her that spirit which will start her on the road to the happy life she desires. Even such a simple prayer as this:

"I am a child of God. I am now filled with His life, strength, health, and power. I am joyous, happy, and enthusiastic about life!"

In the final analysis, there is just one remedy for Lenore's undesirable circumstances—single-mindedness. One of Unity's books, *Divine Remedies*, has this to say about healing heart conditions:

"Greater fearlessness, love, and uprightness

or singleness of mind are necessary for the healing of the heart. . . . To be 'pure in heart' means to be of one purpose, one aim. That one purpose, one aim, above everything else must be to give first place in your life to God and to the work of expressing Him in your every thought, word, and deed. When you seek God with your whole mind, you will find Him. You will be filled with love, and you will become fearless and free. Your heart action will respond; the physical organ and its every function will be strong, vital, and whole."

"If you knew the gift of God," Jesus said to the Samaritan woman at the well, "and who it is that is saying to you, 'Give me a drink,' you would have asked him and he would have given you living water."

Lenore has asked of Him; now she is receptive to the "living water" of healing and understanding. No longer is she drifting, her doubt canceling her desire to believe. Now she is ready to accept the Truth of God, to know His Truth for herself.

Gaining on the
Roundabouts

The English have a charming aphorism: "What you lose on the swings, you gain on the roundabout." My best British friend explains that this originated in the amusement park, whose owner philosophically noted that any loss of income from the swings—a relatively inexpensive amusement device—would be made up from tickets sold to the roundabout (a merry-go-round).

Just how accurate the phrase is as an index to economic experience, I have no way of knowing. But it *is* an interesting maxim, isn't it? "What you lose on the swings, you gain on the roundabout"—it has a lilt and rhythm almost like that of a carrousel!

It is also a pretty good eleven-word explanation of the law of balance and compensation.

There is no such thing as loss without gain, no matter how complete and final the loss may seem to be, if one will make any effort to recoup. However, plucking gain from loss is not done without some conscious, deliberate effort. If the amusement park operator did not have the roundabout operating, with music playing and lights flashing, his loss on the swings would end up as loss—period.

So the law of balance is both reassuring and cautionary. We learn from it that we can make a comeback from any situation or circumstance—but we also learn from it that a comeback is an active, forward movement, not a passive waiting for something to happen.

This points up the necessity of living usefully, instead of just existing. George Bernard Shaw once suggested that every member of civilized society should be required to appear "at reasonable intervals before a properly qualified jury to justify his existence, which should be summarily and painlessly terminated if he fails to justify it." While we would not go along with Shaw's droll cynicism, we would agree that anyone should be able (if called upon) to evaluate his contribution to the world whose bounty he enjoys.

Being good is not a passive thing. One cannot withdraw from active participation in life, and forego all misbehavior, and thus achieve goodness. This is making something negative out of what is essentially, inherently, positive.

Dr. Humphry Osmond, the scientist who coined the word *psychedelic*, said in speaking about the discoveries of our era in the field of medicine: "Why are we all so preoccupied with the pathological, the negative? Is health only the lack of sickness? Is good merely the absence of evil?"

No, we cannot enjoy the good simply by eschewing the evil; we do not enjoy health merely by avoiding sickness. "What you lose on the swings, you gain on the roundabout"—if you keep the roundabout working. If you expect to have a good life, you have to ask yourself what you are willing to do to achieve it . . . and you have to remember, too, that one of the most significant spiritual laws is that we receive in proportion as we give. When we consciously and deliberately bless

83

someone else, either mentally or by our actions, we are blessed.

Often we are able to find honorable excuses for not getting involved deeply in so-called "controversial" matters. But the fact is that each of us has opportunity after opportunity to become involved, if he is willing to recognize these opportunities. (And God teaches us, if we are honest scholars, to know the difference between taking a stand for the good and involving ourselves in a dispute for the sake of the controversy.)

Whatever your reasons might be for not becoming involved in any particular circumstance, don't let yourself be limited because you feel there is "nothing you can do." If you have money, power, influence, so much the better; but if you have none of these, there is still a great deal you can do.

There is someone (probably several persons) who might never be influenced by an advertisement, a news story, a television program . . . but who will listen instantly and intently to *your* views. Make no mistake about it, you *are* a power and an influence in your own world, and it is your privilege and your duty to exert your influence for what you believe to be right. When you do this, of course, you should not expect automatic agreement with your views, even from those who love you best and respect you; but you can know that your views will be considered, and thus you will discharge your obligation to take a meaningful stand. Someone who knows and respects you is waiting and expecting your viewpoint, your opinion; you cannot do less than express it, freely and lovingly.

John Woolman was a clerk in a small store, a member of the Quaker sect, in the early part of the eighteenth century. One day in 1742 he was ordered by his employer to make out a bill of sale for a Negro woman who was being sold to another Quaker. Woolman had a sudden flash of divine illumination which convinced him instantaneously of the evil of slavery—and he dropped everything and devoted the rest of his life to expressing his deep concern about the issue.

He traveled throughout America and Great Britain, speaking simply and sincerely to his fellow Quakers of his conviction that slavery must be eradicated. He gave up eating sugar and wearing cotton clothing because these were produced by slave labor. He was not an intellectual man, and his writing was not brilliant; still it was moving and effective, and it remains a minor American literary classic because (in the words of one of today's critics) it had the "moral quality of humility . . . that elevated it to the level of great prose."

Due almost solely to Woolman's fervor and sincerity, the Society of Friends came to renounce slavery, and became the earliest, most powerful single force in the antislavery movement. Yet all that Woolman did, really, was voice his concern among his friends and associates . . . repeatedly, consistently, sincerely. He had an utter conviction of what he believed, and he shared that belief as widely and as intensely as possible.

Perhaps few of us are given such striking, sudden illumination as that which convinced John Woolman, or Saul on the road to Damascus; but I think that for each one of us, there must be a moment of decision, of choice. I cannot believe that we ever just "slip into" a determined, positive course of action for the good (or in the opposite direction, either). Throughout our life, God sets before us doors to be opened—or disregarded. And often after we have opened one door and walked confidently forward, we find still more doors along the corridor of our growth and progress, and we have the choice of grasping the handles of these and opening them, too. Nor do I believe that there is ever a time when we will find that life is "leveling off," becoming a smooth, bland highway without barriers or detours. This, it seems to me, is one of the great gifts of God: the continuing awareness that there will always be a new opportunity to choose the better way, regardless of how far we have come or how much we have progressed.

How deeply should you and I become involved in the issues and affairs of our time? It is a question that each of us will have to answer individually. You may have better opportunities than I to express your convictions and beliefs; or you may have more compelling reasons for limiting your involvement to certain issues or groups. The best I can hope for you is what I hope for myself: the wisdom and courage to grasp the handle of any door that is there to be opened . . . without letting any risk of loss or disagreement tip the scales, knowing that "what we lose on the swings, we gain on the roundabout."

Seeing Things As We Are

One night I was awakened from sleep by a singing bird. It was an experience I had never had before: to hear in the deep of night, in the midst of a busy city, a bird singing so gloriously that his song woke me.

I have never paid much attention to the songs of birds; they have been part of the "background music" of everyday life, and I couldn't identify one bird from another by its song. But this bird, singing at night, singing with such abandon, such full-throated beauty . . . it was like no other bird I had ever heard! Its song had so much variety, went from trill to warble to chirp, seemingly never repeating a measure, and it went on for almost an hour.

Not one to appreciate being awakened out of sleep, I relaxed and listened, marveling at what beauty there could be in the singing of a bird. I listened, as I had probably never listened before to the music a bird makes.

The next morning I told several friends about my experience, because I was eager to find out what kind of bird, what *rara avis*, might be frequenting this bustling city. I thought surely it must have been a nightingale, wandering far from its accustomed haunts, or some equally little-known bird in our community. But finally one friend smiled understandingly, and said: "No, it wasn't a rare bird at all. It was an ordinary mockingbird."

Further inquiry proved that he was right. The bird whose song made such a great impression on me was one of our more ordinary specimens. Surely I had heard a mockingbird's song before; I've been familiar with mockingbirds since childhood. But *this* mockingbird moved me deeply, because (for one reason or another) I was ready to hear his song.

Now I am wondering how many more of

life's seemingly commonplace experiences will one day move me as deeply, mean as much to me . . . when I am ready to listen, or to see.

We human beings have some strange quirks! We like to think, in these days of instant and almost universal communication, that we share vicariously almost every experience and sensation that the rest of mankind knows. We see a moon landing televised, and we feel that we are almost there on the moon with the astronauts. We enjoy a travelogue, and we tell ourselves that we are really making the journey with the narrator. But . . .

I can remember vividly the first time I stood on the edge of the Grand Canyon. Like everyone else, I had seen picture after picture of the Canyon, all my life. I had been dutifully impressed, I had said to myself, "Yes, it *is* a great scenic spectacle, isn't it?"

But nothing that I had seen in pictures, nothing that I had heard returned travelers tell, had really prepared me for the breathtaking majesty of the Grand Canyon itself, seen and experienced firsthand.

I have had many similar experiences, of finding out how much greater is the reality than the telling about it, and so have you.

Perhaps there is a clue here . . . a suggestion as to why some of the answers seem to elude us.

Recently I heard a speaker say that our next great advance must be in attaining eternal life . . . not in the accepted, "safe" sense that most of us speak of it, but in the very real sense that Charles Fillmore spoke of so often ("This is not a religious question but a matter of life or death; . . . of survival here and now of everybody and everything one holds dear"). For the most part, we have preferred not to face up to this challenge.

"The last enemy to be destroyed is death," Paul said. Did he mean that we must meet all the other challenges before we dare challenge death? Or did he mean that once man destroys this enemy, he will have no other enemies left to face?

It is time we faced up to such questions as these. That we may not find all the answers right away is no reason not to seek them. Until we are willing to begin seeking . . . to begin in earnest, without evasion and without euphemistic halfway measures . . . we aren't going to make much progress.

What does this have to do with my mockingbird in the middle of the night? Well, my experience with the mockingbird indicates to me how much more meaningful and significant any experience can be if I am ready for it. And I have to ask myself, would not a great deal of my life experience become more vital and significant if I were consciously to *make myself* ready for it?

A contemporary poet has said that "We see things not as they are but as we are." A mockingbird's song is movingly beautiful to me when I am receptive to its beauty. When I am loving and giving, those around me are the same, because I see them as I am, not as they are. When I am consciously aware of health and wholeness in my body, I am well and whole, because I am seeing life as I am, not as it seems to be.

You have heard others tell of wonderful healings, marvelous experiences of finding abundance, demonstrating peace and harmony. But until you are consciously ready to experience such things personally . . . until you see life whole, because in your thinking you *are* whole . . . all these things will be merely reported events. When you are *really* ready to see Truth in all about you, it will be there. You will see things as you are, not as they are. You will no longer let facts hide Truth.

Are you ready for a life-shaking experience of your own? All change, all growth, all development is from within, outward. There is nothing to be gained by lamenting unpleasant conditions, complaining about unsatisfactory circumstances. You will see a change for the better when you are ready to change your thinking, your attitude, for the better. Do you say, "I can't change my thinking just by deciding to do it"? Ah, but you can! Not completely at once, not in the twinkling of an eye, but thought by thought, until the transformation is complete.

Just deciding that you want yourself to be different (and better) is a positive action in itself. You may not realize what is happening right away; you may not see any outward changes at once. But then, perhaps, you'll suddenly hear a bird singing . . . and realize that for the first time, you're really *hearing* the song!

Freedom to Seek

Anyone who has been a "Truth student" for any length of time has observed a truly remarkable phenomenon: some of those who are genuinely interested in metaphysical, New Thought teachings are every bit as rigid and immovable as some of those in the so-called orthodox religious movements.

This is a phenomenon because freedom and tolerance and resilience of thought are inherent in the very nature of all metaphysical teachings. Since it would be impolite for us to criticize others for faults we ourselves have, let's narrow this down. For a starting point, we can cite Unity's cofounder, Charles Fillmore:

"In religion is a school of thinkers corresponding to . . . independent physical scientists. They are thinking the problems of life out from an entirely original standpoint. They start with the proposition that there is one Spirit, or one Mind, from which originate all thoughts. They do not allow that any textbook or Scripture is authority for this—that it is Truth, and Truth reveals itself. This one universal Mind, being the only source of intelligence, will inform all those who look to it with undivided attention, and they will know the absolute Truth independent of all authorities who have preceded them."

A careful study of Charles Fillmore's writings will reveal dozens of similar passages in which he emphasizes the open-minded approach to Truth. Those who knew him best remember him as a seeker, not as an all-knowing head of a widespread religious movement. (I have been actively involved in Unity work for nearly a quarter of a century, and I have had close working contact and fellowship with dozens of persons who knew Charles Fillmore as a personal friend; but I have never heard of any instance in which he set himself up as a final authority on any matter of dogma or philosophy. On the other hand, I have heard over and over again how Charles Fillmore said that he "reserved the right to change his mind," because he might believe differently tomorrow than he did today.)

What made Charles and Myrtle Fillmore leaders of thought in their day was their inquiring, seeking attitude. Unity began and grew not as a cult or a sect, but as a loosely knit group of men and women with the same humble yet significant objective: to discover how to make Truth effective in their lives. All those with similar goals were warmly welcomed into fellowship, without restriction or question.

The early issues of *Modern Thought*, predecessor to today's *Unity* Magazine, were open to the theories and speculations of a wide variety of the day's seekers, from spiritualists to graphologists. There would be little point in making today's Unity publications so general in nature; but neither is there much point in making them rigid, unyielding bastions of "Unity thought" to the exclusion of all else.

After all, what is "Unity thought"? If Charles Fillmore refused to state it rigidly and dogmatically, what right have any of us today to do so? The Unity Movement embraces millions of people throughout the world, of almost every religious persuasion. We can hardly say (when Charles Fillmore himself did not) that one must be a Christian to be as open-minded as Unity's founders were in welcoming all who are honestly seeking Truth, in whatever form and in whatever place.

Newton Dillaway says that the least-known passage in the Bible may be this one from the book of Hebrews: "Therefore let us leave the elementary doctrines of Christ and go on to maturity, not laying again a foundation of repentance from dead works." He says that he has never heard these words cited in a pulpit or seen them quoted in any Christian document, because, he feels, "few Christians have ever dared to face the vast implications of this challenging passage."

Dillaway says that if you accept this statement you are "as free as the wind"; you are not bound by any Christian doctrine, you are free to leave behind any doctrine and go on in the way best suited to your own needs, seeking perfection.

Unity came into being at the appropriate

time, for a divine purpose: helping to recast and clarify existing religious theories and doctrines to make them useful and valid for the people of that time. Unity exists today for the same purpose, and it would surely be a denial of our divine plan should we close our thinking to any aspect of the contemporary search for truth.

The point is, of course, that I *need not* agree with anyone else's theories about Truth. Truth itself is immovable and unchangeable, but men approach it by way of innumerable theories and postulations. Because I have a certain theory about how to seek out the truth, and how to put it to work in my affairs, I *must not* therefore deny anyone else the right to advocate an entirely different theory.

For instance, I believe (in general) in reincarnation. I do not understand it fully, of course, but it satisfies many of my uncertainties about what Ernest Wilson calls "the heretofore and the hereafter." So I welcome the theory of reincarnation as a logical, possible answer. But I do not jeer at, or condemn, anyone who believes that after his time on earth is ended he will walk the golden streets of a literal heaven . . . and I don't expect him to scoff at me, either.

I have had firsthand knowledge of enough instances of extrasensory perception and similar psychical phenomena to believe that these little-understood mental powers of mankind may be closer to universal application than they have ever been. I also have many friends who believe that man's trying to tap supramental powers is arrant nonsense. I have other friends who honestly feel that any attempt to tap such powers only inhibits man's ability to "go on to maturity," as the writer to the Hebrews puts it.

Several persons I know and like are seriously interested in astrology; they believe that there is much to be learned by observing the influence of the stars and the planets on men's affairs. Personally I have no serious interest in this field, but I respect the views of those who feel otherwise. They are intelligent, wise persons, and who am I to say that I am wiser than they?

After all, isn't freedom to seek Truth our most precious talent? There is no way we can force others to our way of thinking about anything, even if we wanted to do so. Minds are changed only when there is irresistible evidence that a change is desirable, or necessary. Why would we want it otherwise?

One of the Bible's most reassuring promises is "Seek, and you will find." Jesus did not specify the means of seeking, nor did He insist that a certain goal should be sought; He simply promised that the sincere seeker would reach a goal. It seems, then, that it behooves us to accommodate our own seeking to that of everyone else, to welcome as "fellow travelers" all who are seeking along any road.

There is a familiar hymn (an old one, I am sure) by William Bradbury, which sings of those who are "united in the Truth . . . one in the freedom of the Truth . . . one in the joy of paths untrod . . . one in the larger thought of God." The hymn's finest line is: "The seekers of the Light are one."

When we seek, we *are* one with every seeker, whether we know it or not. If the word *unity* has any meaning at all, surely that is its grandest meaning: the oneness of all who seek the Truth. So we cannot turn away from, or condemn, or criticize those who are seeking along different lines from our own . . . because we would only be condemning our-

101

self. If we have the right to test the theories that we think will lead us to the Truth, everyone else has the same right. Perhaps it is time we reaffirmed this universal right, lest we begin to restrict our own freedom to seek.

The Truth about Losing

Imagine a spaceship from another solar system, cruising in the starry reaches of our universe. The occupants see a medium-size planet, and the ship is headed toward it. They come within some five hundred miles of the planet, but can observe no signs of life. In fact, they can see no evidence that the planet is inhabited, or had ever known any form of intelligent life: no highways, no buildings, no construction of any kind.

This was an exercise of imagination. However, it was based on what our own astronauts saw as their ship orbited the earth, at an altitude of four or five hundred miles. They could see no evidence that the earth was or ever had been inhabited by intelligent creatures.

So much for appearances . . . for the "evidence" of our senses!

We have all had many instances of seeing something that was not really as our vision delineated it, or of not seeing what was there all the time. In short, we *know* that appearances are not to be relied on. Why, then, do we overlook this truth in so much of our thinking?

Most of us seldom have the experience of "losing" quite as definitively as a political candidate who is not elected to the office he seeks. But we do sometimes lose out on some desired attainment, or some wanted relationship with another person does not turn out as we hoped it would . . . and usually such losses affect us strongly. When we examine a loss, as the astronauts peered at the earth hundreds of miles below, we tend to see only our disappointment and frustration . . . but this is an illusory view.

"All right," someone may say, "so the astronauts could see no evidence of life on the earth. A scientist would not be satisfied with just viewing the earth with the naked eye, five hundred miles away in space; he would insist on using a high-powered telescope, to make sure."

Quite true . . . but are we not scientists, too? Are we not scientists in the life of the spirit . . . and shouldn't we, too, use all of the insight and illumination we can get to find the truth of the matter, when it comes to loss or defeat?

A scientist knows that a naked-eye view of something hundreds of miles distant is not a reliable view. We know that disappointment in loss is no less unreliable, as an intelligent reaction and response.

An essay in Time magazine suggests that there must be "such a thing as the art of losing well." The writer says, "Most of the authenticated sages—quite a few losers among them—emphasize a very ancient idea: because the loser alone controls his attitude, he can always change that attitude and regard defeat as unimportant. 'Our life,' said Marcus Aurelius, the Roman emperor-philosopher, 'is what our thoughts make it.' "

It is virtually impossible for the average person to anticipate accurately the ultimate success or failure of all (or even most) of his plans and projects. Even with the best intentions, and with the most positive, optimistic viewpoint, a man cannot predict every outcome. An attitude of positive determination to achieve is certainly a factor in achievement; but, because we cannot know all the factors involved, we cannot be sure of anything except the fact that, whatever happens, "God meant it for good."

Curiously enough, it is *because* we cannot be sure of the outcome of any given situation that we should cultivate and maintain a positive, cheerful attitude. God does intend only good for us, so we should not let the imponderables make us pessimistic or negative.

Another illustration from a recent election is useful: Near the close of the campaigns, the public-opinion surveys showed that the leading candidates had captured the favor of nearly equal numbers of potential voters. In fact, the candidates were so close in percentage points that the pollsters said that the election was "too close to call." This is often true of our affairs—the factors involved are such that there is no way for us to "call" the ultimate turn of events. All we can do—and what we should do—is hold to our firm belief in a good outcome, without insisting (even mentally) that every detail be worked out exactly as we have decided it should be.

Defeat, says one writer, is a better teacher than success . . . simply because defeat, if we react to it in the right way, is a humbling and a corrective process. When we lose—in achievement, in human relations, in anything—we need to break with some of the practices which have been holding us back and causing defeat. So the true value of losing is that it forces us to think about why we lost.

Losing is never better than winning, of course. But until we achieve perfection, we may as well get some good out of losing. It is absurd to believe that God causes our defeats and losses "to teach us a lesson"; God's lessons for living are taught in achieving and attaining. But there *is* a definite good to be derived from losing, and it is this: losing (if we let it) can cause us to discover what we have left.

In the divine scheme of things, no loss is ever final or complete. When we lose, we should think not about what was, or what might have been, but about what still can be.

The failure of some project, or the unsatisfactory evolvement of some relationship, is (like success) arriving at a certain stage of our development. We grow—physically, mentally, spiritually—by stages; we reach one level and go on to another. Whether we reach that level by succeeding or failing, it *is* a level of growth. Our further evolvement depends on what we do once that level has been reached. If we have lost something we expected to win, we can accept the loss as irretrievable, or we can use it to develop a new philosophy of winning.

"If you know these things, blessed are you if you do them." We *know* that the appearance of loss and defeat and failure is just that, an appearance. If we *do* what we know we should do, when we lose or fail, we will be truly blessed . . . and we turn defeat to triumph. What is required is a sure faith in the ultimate outworking of good.

"Count Me In"

A few years ago, a book was compiled of letters children had written to God. All of the letters were fresh, charming, and often touching because they represented the simple, uncomplicated thinking that children bring to such things.

One of the most impressive letters in the collection consists of just six words:

"Dear God:

Count me in.

Herbie."

What was Herbie trying to say? We can only speculate, but it seems likely that he had been told about God and His good plans for the world, and that he was simply stating his own desire to be included in those plans. Perhaps his parents, or a Sunday-school teacher, had explained to Herbie that God needs the help of all His children in making His plans a reality—and Herbie was expressing his personal faith in all this by saying to God, "Count me in."

How fine it would be if each of us could say to God, promptly and emphatically, "Count me in!"

Yet how often do we say, either in what we do or in what we do not do: "God, I'm all in favor of what You're doing in this particular area, but——I'd rather not get involved. It's a little controversial, God, so if You don't mind, I'll stay out of it."

One of the criticisms we "good people" have had leveled at us (and often justifiably) is that we have been afraid of getting involved in many of the great issues of our time. Although many as individuals have involved themselves in some of the controversies between right and wrong, as a body we have all too often preferred to stay on the side-lines. Ours is a spiritual work, we say apologetically (and how revealing that word *apolo-*

110

getically is!); if we get into controversial matters, we may lose our spiritual effectiveness.

Of course we have no historical justification for feeling this way. Christianity was a controversial movement from its very beginning. The early leaders of the Christian church were personally and collectively involved with all kinds of governmental and political controversies, and rightly so.

Jesus Himself was probably the most controversial figure of His time and place; because He knew that His message was true, He stoutly withstood all official efforts to silence Him. He, and many of His followers, gave up life itself because of their involvement in the most controversial issues of their day.

All of the growth and progress of Christianity has come about through the efforts of leaders who were not afraid to take their stand for what they believed to be true. In fact, all of mankind's progress and growth stems from the leadership of "involved" men and women who refused to believe that controversy is of itself harmful.

Few of us are ever asked to give up life itself for what we believe in today—but we *are* required to take a stand. And there has been a refreshing change among believers of all faiths in the last few years—a movement toward active involvement in the problems and challenges of everyday living.

At last we are coming to understand what a few dedicated persons in every age have known: that it is not only possible but *essential* for good people to become involved in every facet of life; that spiritual involvement is truly the forerunner for active, and very personal involvement.

There can be no doubt about it: if a cause— any cause, spiritual, political, or other—be truly right and good, then I owe that cause my personal involvement in it, my support of it.

It is not enough for me to believe, and perhaps mention to a few of my friends, that I hold a certain point of view in some matter of moral or ethical importance. I must give my open, public support to that point of view. I cannot in good conscience remain uninvolved, no matter how much my becoming involved may upset my normal way of life.

There are, of course, different ways of

becoming involved, of "counting myself in" among those who stand for Truth. First of all I must be quite sure where my deepest sympathies and strong convictions lie—and then I must stand up and be counted on that side, whether the issue is great or small.

The most important things in our life today are almost inevitably controversial, to some degree. (Marcus Bach brings this out emphatically in his book *The Challenge of Change*, in which he makes it wonderfully clear that in every so-called crisis that confronts us, there is both challenge and opportunity.)

Involvement itself is basic. It may be either active or passive, as long as it is clear and unmistakable. The soldier who believes that a military cause is just takes his stand by his military services, just as the conscientious objector or the peace marcher states his position (by his actions) against military solutions.

Of course it matters what position is right— but for the individual, honestly seeking the truth, what matters most is that he supports what he *believes* to be right.

One of the wonderful truths about our involvement is that Spirit always guides. We are guided to make right decisions—and we are guided to know just what we should do to support and strengthen those decisions. Best of all, we are led to do whatever we do in love, with genuine respect for the ideas and actions of others with whom we may not agree.

"To discern the truth . . . and to prove it." What a magnificent task lies before us! It is an objective to which we would willingly devote our thinking and our believing—but will we also take the trouble to become personally, actively involved in it?

Surely you feel, as I do, that we can no longer afford the luxury of avoiding controversy. Where there is controversy, it exists because the right is challenging the wrong. In some instances, my idea of what is right may not agree wholly with yours; but in the great majority of cases, I will *know* which is the right side, as you will; and I want to be on that side, so completely and firmly that no one can doubt where I stand. If I see that a good cause needs my support, I want to give support. I want to be a part of truth and goodness.

Dear God: Count me in.

Involvement

You can search the Bible from Genesis to Revelation without finding the word *involvement*, or any variation of it. The massive 1,003-page Oxford Dictionary of Quotations cites just one usage: in Donne's famous line,

"Any man's death diminishes me, because I am involved in Mankind."

It seems clear that *involvement* is definitely a "modern" word, at least as we normally use it. Indeed, Webster's Seventh New Collegiate Dictionary gives no definitions for "involve" that suggest its contemporary usage.

Perhaps some contemporary philologist has traced the evolution of the word in its current meaning. In any event, we have only to think of contemporary synonyms for "involvement"—participation, sharing, and so on—to realize that the word's present-day meaning is a familiar one and has been for centuries, in one form or another.

Involvement is almost never a "neutral" word. Some people think of involvement as commendable acceptance of high responsibility. Others think of it as worrisome complication. What is more, it is usually an "action" word: it denotes doing something, taking a stand, declaring oneself.

We have read news stories of personal attacks in large cities that are observed by bystanders, who do nothing to help the victims because they do not want to "get involved." Or we are exhorted by civic leaders, politicians, and others to "get involved" in the important issues of our time, to "stand up and be counted" among supporters of various causes and projects.

At least one thing can be said for involvement, in personal matters or larger affairs: it signifies sincerity and honest interest. Regardless of the cause they support, leaders seldom if ever suggest that others join them casually.

What is wanted is honest, dedicated participation . . . *involvement* . . . stemming from
inner leading or inspiration. (It is interesting
to note that "involve" is from a Middle
English root word meaning "to roll up;
wrap." One who is genuinely involved in anything is in effect "wrapped up" in it.)

Some who would like to support certain
principles or ideas are reluctant to become
"involved," because to them involvement
signifies some kind of militant stand . . .
protest, opposition, etc. Actually we can
become sincerely and effectively involved in
any issue or cause on the spiritual level—and
that is where our involvement should begin
always.

We involve ourselves in the challenges and
the opportunities of others when we have
genuine concern for them, when we care
about them and what happens to them . . .
first "move" we make in any kind of involvement must be prayer—which is in fact the
deepest involvement of all. When we care
deeply enough about a person or a situation
to pray fervently, we are given guidance along
the line of any other steps we should take.
But prayer is the first, and the most powerful,

form of involvement open to us.

Nor should we ever think of involvement only as taking part in challenging affairs, taking a stand on one side or the other in a controversial situation. Involvement can be all this . . . but in its simplest form, involvement is best described in Donne's words: "I am involved in Mankind." We are all part of mankind, and whatever affects any man affects each of us. Whatever we do affects everyone else in the human race, in some way, in some measure. And because this is true, how we approach each day's living is a measure of the extent of our involvement with life.

Eric Butterworth wrote a book entitled *Life Is for Living.* "Life is not for existing, or 'waiting for something to turn up,' " he says. "What would you think of an airline pilot who rolled his plane out onto the runway and roared up into the sky, and then, at the proper cruising speed and altitude, released the controls and settled back in his seat, saying, 'Well, I wonder where the plane will go today?' "

Yet this is the way many persons approach life, Butterworth goes on: they begin the day with the thought, "Well, I wonder what this day is going to bring?" Such an approach rules out any real involvement with mankind, with the universe, with God. It is equivalent to taking a permanent seat on the sidelines, observing, applauding sometimes, criticizing often, but never really participating, never "playing the game."

The happy people are those who are involved with living. Sometimes we think of "contentment" as meaning a kind of smug, restful withdrawing from action, whereas in reality the contented person is the one who has achieved an understanding of life. Webster says (brilliantly) that one who is content "is not disturbed or disquieted even though every wish is not fully realized." That kind of self-knowledge can come only from full participation in life, from involvement.

It is essential (to you and to everyone) that you be involved every day of your life. The extent and nature of your involvement will almost certainly not be the same as mine, but that is not the important thing. The very *fact* of your involvement is the key point . . . for you, and for the rest of the world. You must keep everlastingly in mind the truth that your

119

decision to be involved, reaffirmed daily, even hourly, does make a difference to mankind.

"What we need to remember," said J. L. Keith, "is that the 'march of nations' is simply the movement of individuals toward a common goal. What each individual does has its own special meaning, its own place in the fabric of history. What *you* do is important. In fact, the action of the individual is the greatest force in any age. . . .

"Human life and progress is knit of a million tiny stitches, each one locking into many others. Wherever there is a dropped stitch or a faulty one, the fabric is flawed; but where each tiny stitch is true and strong, the fabric is perfect."

Certainly it can not be emphasized too much that involvement is not necessarily a matter of taking a controversial stand. In his definitive book *The Unity Way of Life*, Marcus Bach says, "When Unity members get just as upset with the world as does anyone else . . . then Unity has lost its meaning." But why should our seeing the need for change and improvement upset us?

I have sometimes wondered why it is that we who call ourselves "Truth students" so often deny the Truth about unpleasant situations and conditions. How can we explain the fact that when we are faced with a momentary crisis, we may forget everything we know about Truth and reach out to press the panic button?

We don't believe in controversy for the sake of controversy, and certainly we believe that Unity's basic purpose is to express and teach the healing principles of Jesus Christ. The thing is, though, that in many instances these healing principles need to be applied to some of today's most "controversial" problems, even though they may be problems that do not affect you and me personally. A war in Asia may not affect me or any member of my family individually; but it affects the world I live in, the country I live in, the community I live in, so it affects me, and I cannot be a good Truth student if I refuse to think about it and do whatever I can to give substance to my feelings about it.

There is no reason why thinking about mankind's problems and challenges should depress us or upset us. Rather, such thinking should fill us with optimism, because we *know* there is a way out, a solution, an opportunity where there seems to be a problem.

We will surely agree that every achievement and every solution evolves from an idea. So what we should pray for, when we feel threatened in any way, is the right idea . . . the idea that will help us see the way out. There *is* a way out, of that we are sure; but it is sometimes obscured by our fear and worry. So if at first glance we can't see the way out, we need to pray, simply and earnestly, for illumination . . . vision to see the necessary solution.

Ideas are not hard to come by, if we can quiet our anxious thoughts and concentrate on the positive possibilities. This calls for controlled thinking, something we lazily neglect to insist on most of the time. (It's so easy to let the mind ramble, without direction!) Careless thinking is a luxury we can't really afford, and we learn this when our thoughts become filled with ominous portents of trouble and doom.

Once we decide to control our thinking, and consciously seek the idea or answer that embodies our good, it's only a matter of time until we find it. Surely this is one of the ways in which we benefit from the less-than-good:

it forces us to take charge of our thoughts.

It is a mark of spiritual maturity to be able to view any situation and see good in it instead of evil. It is a mark of spiritual weakness to refuse to think about what needs to be done to replace the many illnesses of the human race with the wholeness of God. It takes courage, and we have to be firmly grounded in Truth, if we are to use the power of our thought to help right unsatisfactory conditions. But unless we can do this without getting upset with the world, then the Truth we say we believe in hasn't really touched us deeply.

Beauty in Desert Places

A desert is (to many people) a vast, endless, monotonous expanse of earth and sky, sparsely scattered with spindly vegetation . . . dry, uninteresting, even boring. But to many others, a desert is a wonderful, beautiful place, more appealing than mountain or grassy plain.

To some travelers a desert is a threatening area to be traversed, something to be gotten through as quickly as possible. To others—those with air-conditioned automobiles, or those traveling in luxurious trains or planes—a desert is simply one stage in a journey, as easily and as pleasantly crossed as any other area.

The difference, in each instance, is in preparation and adjustment. One who expects to be crossing a desert wisely prepares for the journey, perhaps by taking along extra water if he plans to travel afoot, or by making sure that his transportation is equipped to withstand desert temperatures and conditions. If one anticipates living in a desert, he does whatever he can to make his surroundings comfortable, and then he deliberately sets out to acclimate himself to desert living. The traveler who defies the desert, or the person who resigns himself to desert living with no expectation of satisfaction or pleasure, finds the desert unpleasant and frightening.

Deserts sometimes symbolize the arid, discouraging spaces in our life. (This would not be true for one who had adjusted to actual desert living, of course.) These "dry spots" aren't always unpleasant, or threatening; they are simply periods of seeming monotony, when our life seems to be a matter of routine without change.

Some people, of course, find routine the better way of life. You may hunger for excitement and out-of-the-ordinary happenings, but I may find security and peace of mind in day-by-day living that is more or less on schedule, structured in familiar ways. Again, it is in many ways a matter of preparation and adjustment. If your normal way of life is such that high adventure seems out of the picture, you should find a different kind of adventure in everyday happenings. Routine need not be boring or frustrating, any more than desert living need be dull and tiresome. However, when we hear the word *routine* we usually glimpse a quick image of boredom and monotony. Since most of us inevitably spend a great deal of our time in routine situations, the best thing we can do is prepare for such living . . . as we would prepare for traveling or living in a desert place.

One of the best ways of preparing is learning to understand the purposes and the uses of the "desert spaces" in life.

The Bible makes many references to desert (or wilderness) places. Often the desert was a place of renewal, of growth, as it was for Jesus and for John the Baptist. Whether it is thought of as a geographical entity or a symbolical period of time, the desert has frequently been a valuable, not-to-be-missed experience for men throughout history. Going apart, to find inspiration, relaxation or insight, can be wonderfully uplifting . . . if one does not stay apart, but returns to share what he has found.

The vital thing to remember about those who "went apart" into deserts of space or time, and came out refreshed and invigorated, is that they did so knowingly, deliberately, even eagerly. They were prepared for their desert experience.

There are countless instances of wealthy, successful men and women who recall with distinct pleasure their early "desert experiences." Many a young couple has entered into marriage with seemingly inadequate resources and, because they were determined to make their love live, found in those early, lean years a kind of deep, inner pleasure that built a foundation for all the rest of their life together. They were prepared to travel safely and happily through a dry period, and they did.

It is important to know, too, that any desert experience, no matter how routine or even risky it seems to be, cannot be without its moments of beauty and pleasure. They rise before your eyes as the flowering cactus rises out of desert sands.

Coming upon beauty, even adventure, in everyday routine is not a matter of faith, so much as it is a matter of acceptance, awareness. Driving through the desert, the traveler need not have faith that he will see the glowing bloom of a cactus; all he needs to know is that such beauty exists in the desert, and all he has to do is be prepared to see it when he comes upon it. Instead of driving on grimly, eyes straight ahead, straining to complete the journey, he can let his thoughts (and his vision) stray to take in all his surroundings . . . and eventually, perhaps out of the corner of an eye, he will see the desert's incomparable flower.

The beauty, the extraordinary pleasure we encounter in our ordinary days, may take the form of a casual friendship formed with someone else who is also crossing his "desert place" in life. Shared experiences always make for strong bonds . . . and these experiences need not be harrowing or critical; friendships that spring up between persons who share the monotony of a particular kind of work are sometimes long-lasting and vital. The only obstacle to finding such relationships is the wall we can erect between ourself and our surroundings.

Blinders are for horses; men and women have no need of them, nor any use for them. You are the sole driver of your life-vehicle, and you will reach your destination sooner, with more pleasure along the way, if you are completely aware of everything about you. If you know where you are going, and if you are prepared to meet desert conditions as well as mountaintops and smooth highways, your journey will be rewarding every mile of the way.

What's In It for You ?

It is a normal human trait to seek individual benefit in every event of life. Although the attitude is sometimes expressed in the slightly cynical query, "What's in it for me?" it is not (basically) a cynical or selfish attitude. It is natural and right that we should seek some personal benefit from anything that happens to us ... and that we should be cautious about entering upon a new experience without finding out whether or not it will be good for us.

An Oriental philosopher has put into these words one of the familiar and pivotal principles of life: "What is most important to you is not so much the circumstances of your life as your attitude toward them."

While it is necessary that we approach future experiences, whatever they may be, with faith that they contain something of our good, it is perhaps equally important that we recognize and accept the good that we found in past experiences . . . experiences which may have seemed less than good when they came to us.

We are repeatedly advised to "look for the good" in whatever happens, and usually the good is not too hard to find, if we honestly believe that it can be found. However, there are experiences in everyone's life that are so harsh, so upsetting, that it seems almost impossible to find any good in them. Often we go through such experiences virtually in a state of shock, able to do no more than live through them. But of course we do come out again, into the sunlight and the warmth of God's love and protection . . . and it is then (usually) that we begin asking ourself, "But why did I have to go through that? What did I gain from the experience? What was in it for me?"

Of course we are not likely, at this stage of

our growth, to explain away our hardships on the theory that "God is teaching us a lesson." God does not send any particular experience our way; we invite or permit certain experiences to come into our life (perhaps knowingly, perhaps not). God does not use unpleasant experiences to teach us something, but surely He expects that we will find, in every experience, something that contributes to our soul growth.

I have often searched, as you probably have, for the positive good in unhappy experiences. Once when the answer seemed to elude me at length, I finally realized in a flash of insight that a particularly "bad" experience had left me no better off physically, financially, or in any material way . . . but that I had gained in compassion and understanding through the experience.

I have found, too, that it is not always wise, or even necessary, to insist on knowing "what was in it for me." The important thing, of course, is to be quite sure within oneself that whatever happened, God did mean it for good. If I can keep believing this, eventually the good will be revealed to me.

(Nor should we limit our faith in good

133

results to the unpleasant experiences! Often we are prone to accept the good events with a trace of, "Oh, that was fine!" without any real comprehension of just how fine it was. Charles Fillmore writes of the German astronomer who, realizing all at once the perfect order and harmony of the universe, exclaimed in delighted understanding, "O God, I am thinking Thy thoughts after Thee!" This was surely the greatest good the man could have received, but how many of us are aware of this kind of good when we study and learn?)

In one of his charming stories about the Princes of Serendip, Marcus Bach explains that the Princes had three answers to the eternal question, "Why did it happen?" The first answer was, "It happened either for your growth or for your guidance." This is the answer that most of us accept almost unconsciously, if we are rooted and grounded in the goodness of God. We know instinctively that whatever happened, there *must* have been something in it for our growth or guidance.

The Princes' second answer was in the nature of an explanation rather than an answer: "What happened, happened because you drew the happening to yourself by conscious or unconscious forces within yourself." This too we accept, generally speaking, though it is sometimes a "hard saying." It is difficult for us to admit that we are individually responsible for some of the things that come to us (indeed, for all that comes to us), even though we know it is true that "we have only ourself to blame."

And the third answer that the Princes gave was this: "What happened, happened not for your benefit, but for the benefit and profit of someone else."

We know, of course, that we do not live for ourself alone. Our life is inevitably linked to the lives of many, many others. It is not outside the realm of possibility that some of the crises that we face are even more critical to someone else whose life we touch, than to us individually. In other words, although it is always true that experiences come to us through our own thoughts and actions, it is quite possible that our reaction to experiences, and particularly the way in which we come through them, can be of world-shaking import to someone else. We will learn and grow too ... but the experience's prime impact may be on another. And for this, we should be eternally grateful.

What's in it for you? Whatever you find in it . . . and even if you don't find anything at first, you can be sure that the good is there, and that it is already yours. We don't always know exactly what form our good is taking, or just how we are growing in consciousness. It isn't necessary that we know. All that is necessary is that we believe, and accept, without recriminations or resentment. Living through something unpleasant is not enough in itself; we have to *come through*, by putting the unpleasantness firmly behind us and knowing that good is its only residue.

Dreams and the Dreamer

A few years ago the tragic assassination of one of America's leaders brought to our attention a little known verse from Genesis:

"And they said to one another, Behold, this dreamer cometh. Come now therefore, and let us slay him . . . and we shall see what will become of his dreams."

The quotation is from the story of Joseph, whose brothers attempted to kill him because his dreams had seemingly made him their father's favorite. The attempt was not successful.

Of course destroying the dreamer does not necessarily affect "what will become of his dreams" (except that it may make a martyr of him, and thus hasten the realization of those dreams). A great many wise and courageous dreamers have lost their lives for their dreams, but these would represent only a fraction of those who have dreamed and lived to see their dreams come true.

It may be, in fact, that dreamers have a greater life expectancy than nondreamers, if only because the dreamer has a finer grasp of life's potentialities, and thus lives life more fully. Throughout history, the "giant steps for mankind" have been taken by dreamers, because all truly great accomplishment depends on vision and faith.

In a world that we sometimes think of as "hard" and "practical," it may be fashionable to speak of dreamers as impractical visionaries with heads in the clouds. The truth is that dreamers (more than most unimaginative persons) have their feet solidly planted on the ground, and the best of them (whether they be poets, artists, or leaders of nations) find in their dreams the motivation and inspiration to *do*.

The nineteenth-century poet Arthur W. E. O'Shaughnessy wrote movingly:

"We are the music makers,
　　　We are the dreamers of dreams, . . .
　　We are the movers and shakers
　　　Of the world for ever, it seems."

Who has ever aspired to anything higher than being among the "movers and shakers of the world"? And who has ever moved or shaken the world, or any part of it, without the aspirations of dreams and visions?

A respected Biblical authority, writing about dreams and dreamers as mentioned in Scripture, mentions that despite the fact that dreams had a magical connotation to many Eastern peoples, "God revealed His will frequently in dreams, and there were those who could explain them." Joseph, of course, is the first name to come to mind when one recalls Biblical accounts of dreams and dreamers; his whole life was bound up in dreams and how he interpreted them. Charles Fillmore remarks that "Joseph as imagination molds mind substance in the realm of forms. . . . An interpreter of dreams, the phenomenal was his field of action. This formative power is characteristic of the imagination, and among the twelve primal faculties of mind we find that this faculty of the imagination is represented

139

by Joseph."

The words *dream* and *dreamer* are among those which usage seems to have corrupted. Too often they have a fanciful, unreal quality to the average person. But as Charles Fillmore points out, dreaming is simply an activity of the faculty of imagination, something that everybody possesses. "The home of the imagination is in the realm of ideas, where another dimension of mind is opened to it, even the kingdom of the heavens. The imaging faculty gives man the ability to project himself through time and space and thus rise above these limitations as well as all other limitations. Even when the conscious mind is asleep the imagination continues its activity and we have dreams."

Of course dreams have reality only when we awaken. Whether we dream in slumber, or daydream, our imagination is presenting us with ideas, solutions, suggestions, and it is up to us to give these form and substance when we are alert and awake. Because we usually make little if any effort to hold on to our dreams or fantasies, they slip away. (All of us have had the experience of waking in the morning with mere fragments of the night's

dreaming just dissolving in our consciousness.)
And of course many of our dreams and
fantasies are self-induced, by the events of the
day or by our thoughts as we drifted into
sleep. We would not want to keep all these in
our waking mind; they would crowd out
everything else!

But there are plenty of authenticated
accounts of those who have made a conscious
effort to recall their dreams, and have often
succeeded. Scientists now believe that some
of our dreams have much to tell us, about the
past or the future, and that cultivating skill in
fleshing out these dreams holds much promise
for man's greater mental development.

Because we may have little respect for
dreams as such, many of us neglect the power
there is in dreaming. It is important to
remember that all of us dream, much or little,
and it is no one's fault but our own if the
dreaming we do is vague and unproductive.
"Every dream has origin in thought," said
Charles Fillmore, "and every thought makes a
mind picture."

All that is or will be originates as an idea;
until we get an idea, we get nothing. By
receiving and giving form to the ideas that

God's universe has for us, we achieve, we heal, we find solutions, we "move and shake" the earth.

Kipling's famous line states the condition: "If you can dream—and not make dreams your master." Dreaming is not to be regarded as an end in itself, but as a technique for achievement. When we dream, we have to sort out our dreams and select those to which we want to give substance. This is one of the most vital exercises of our precious gift of choice.

Whether or not you develop the technique of recalling the dreams that come to you in sleep is not nearly so important as cultivating the skill of daydreaming . . . consciously letting your waking mind move alertly through the fantasies and possibilities that will populate your thoughts if you let them. Your dreams, especially your daydreams, can have a life and substance that will change your life, if you give your conscious thought to them. If you are seeking a solution, a healing, increased abundance, or any good thing, ask God for an idea—then dream. Be bold enough to sit back, relax, and let your imagination take over. Once you perfect this technique (and it is really one of the simplest, easiest ways of praying), you will own the key to the vault in which all the universe's rich ideas are hidden. But they will not be hidden to you, once you realize what can come through your dreaming.

Everyday Inspiration

What makes you think you're not inspired?

Are you one of those who thinks that inspiration is a divine gift for the few—poets, artists, musicians, and the like? Do you think of inspiration as something above and beyond the average, everyday sort of person . . . like you and me?

If you do, you're wrong.

No matter who you are, you receive inspiration dozens of times a day. You are inspired hour by hour. Every time you get an idea, you are being inspired. Because that is what inspiration is: the divine process by which ideas flow into men's minds.

145

Because ideas are the source of all the wisdom that the universe offers to mankind, all of us would like to become more receptive to ideas. We would like to find surer techniques for getting ideas and putting them to work. And there *are* such techniques.

Several years ago, in my book *The Right Answer* I listed four steps in the idea-getting process. I named these steps *invitation, inspiration, ideation,* and *incubation.* Recently I discovered that a writer named Wallas, hitherto unknown to me, had years ago stated the four stages, which he named *preparation, incubation, illumination,* and *verification.* The nature of the four steps appears to be quite similar, whatever they are named (which is only another of the thousands upon thousands of instances in which nearly identical ideas come to persons totally unrelated and unknown to each other).

It seems certain that all who have thought about the ideating process would agree that a preliminary period—whether it is called "invitation" or "preparation"—is essential. This period may cover many differing mental acts, but they are all simply a matter of "getting ready to be inspired." There is seldom such a thing as inspiration "like a flash from the blue." What seems to be sudden, unexpected inspiration comes usually as a delayed result of earlier preparation.

One of the ways we prepare for inspiration is by asking questions. If we have a problem to solve, a situation to meet, an opportunity to accept, we should ask ourself (our inner Self) just what it is that we expect to accomplish. Then we should become quiet, stop thinking about the problem, and let God ask us questions.

Many of the great scientific discoveries have resulted from seemingly incredible questions which popped into the minds of researchers and thinkers. A long-unsolved scientific mystery occupies the mind of a dedicated scientist; the universe begins putting questions into his mind: "*What if* this were true?" "*What if* this supposedly impossible theory could be proved?" If there are enough questions like these, questions exciting enough to encourage deep thought and research, the scientist begins to find answers . . . in some cases answers previously thought to be impossible.

One philosopher has said that "we hear

only the question to which we are capable of finding an answer." Which is simply another way of saying, no doubt, that "whatever man can conceive, he can achieve."

Once the questions come, and once the answers begin to be sought out, things begin to happen. In many cases (probably in most cases) results come in fairly orthodox, everyday ways: a complicated series of mathematical equations furnishes the needed answer, for instance. But there are plenty of documented instances of seemingly miraculous inspiration.

The Quarternion Theory, a vital part of modern mathematics, "happened to" a University of Dublin professor, Sir William Rowan Hamilton. As he and his wife were walking across a Dublin bridge one morning, as Hamilton describes it, "the galvanic circuit of thought closed," and the fundamental equations that made up his now-famous theory took shape in his mind. And at the moment of inspiration, Hamilton says that he had a sudden understanding that he would need another ten or fifteen years of his life to translate the theory completely into usable form.

148

A "bolt from the blue," we say. But . . . in a letter he wrote soon after his inspiration on the bridge, Hamilton said that this long-cherished notion had "haunted" him for some fifteen years. In other words, the universe had posed a question to him, and when he had sorted everything out in his conscious mind, the solution came as a "sudden" inspiration.

Arnold Toynbee, the famous historian, has recorded an apparently mystical experience he had on Buckingham Palace Road. There, he said, he found himself in communion with all history—"all that had been, and was, and was to come"—and this knowledge flowed through him like a mighty current, giving him the insight and understanding that led to his widely accepted historical writings.

Many have mentioned the inspiration which Albert Einstein acknowledged as the beginning of his theory of relativity. One writer says, "He never doubted that he had been privileged to glimpse into the very mathematical mind and physical heart of all things."

There are even recorded instances of astounding visions that furnished proof of scientific theory. Professor Kekule, the

German chemist who conceived the theory of the benzene ring (which has been called one of the most important theories in modern chemistry) said that he actually "saw" the ring in visual image, clearly and distinctly.

What such records mean to most of us is simply this: The answers are available, if we care enough to ask the questions . . . or, to put it another way, if we care enough to let the universe put questions to us, we can expect to receive the answers too.

But, you say, all this has to do with scientists, writers . . . just the sort of "geniuses" to whom inspiration always comes! True, the instances reported here happened to famous men . . . but that is only because famous men get their "happenings" recorded. You could think of similar experiences of inspiration—less important to the world, perhaps, but just as important to you—that have occurred in your own life.

The salesman who cares enough about doing a good job to think about his sales techniques, to revise and adapt his approach to buyers, to find new and better ways to be useful to his customers . . . that salesman will from time to time be "inspired" to say just the right thing, take just the right tack, and his success will grow.

The housewife to whom cooking is an important part of life will constantly seek out new recipes, new ways to serve familiar dishes, and so on. Because she questions (and because she knows that her job is as vital as that of the scientist) she receives inspiration that results in always-improving meals to nourish and please her family. (Would you dare deny that a superbly baked chocolate cake is inspired?)

This could all be thought of, to put it in contemporary terms, as "letting the sunshine in." No illumination enters the closed mind; no inspiration lifts one who is grounded by resentment and negativism. So the first step . . . whether you wish to call it "invitation" or "preparation" . . . is really just a matter of deciding that you are going to "let the sunshine in."

Accept the wisdom of the universe . . . let God know you're ready to be inspired. Then relax, listen for His questions . . . and watch for His answers!

The Rest of Your Life

A recently-popular song has as its title a phrase that is being rather widely used, especially by young people: "Today is the first day of the rest of your life."

Not too long ago a favorite phrase on church bulletin boards (and one still to be found in some places, no doubt) was "Where are you going to spend eternity?" It's a rather chilling, foreboding question, certainly meant as a warning rather than a message of hope. How much better, then, if the question is rephrased: "Where and how are you going to spend the rest of your life?"

The Christian religion is basically a religion

of forgiving, of redemption; but somehow men have often tried to place limits and restrictions on this. The orthodox church has said, in so many words: "Yes, God forgives your sins ... but final forgiveness is part of life after death. You must not expect to escape punishment; you must pay a penalty for your sins, and later, when God feels you have paid enough, He will call you home and you will be free of all guilt."

If there is one "giant leap forward" that Unity and the other Truth teachings have made possible for mankind, it is in emphasizing the truth that forgiveness is instant and enduring ... that "the rest of your life" can in fact be an entirely new life, regardless of the past. Truth is truly the doctrine of beginning again, of a new start, today and every day as long as you want it to be so.

More than thirty years ago Frank B. Whitney wrote a book called *Beginning Again.* It is still in print, still widely read. The book's lasting appeal can be explained by what the author says in the first chapter:

"The one desire of all men is to feel that they can begin anew, that they can greet each new day with the feeling of new life, that they can feel the urge to press forward when things would seemingly retard them."

And we might add, the one realization that comes to each one who grasps and understands Truth is that beginning again *is* possible . . . not only possible, but inevitable! We become aware that this is true the moment we begin to put into practice the principles of love that we learn. We find out that not only does God forgive our mistakes, our so-called sins, but that our fellowmen are usually equally forgiving.

Man's capacity for forgiving and forgetting is nearly incredible. Ask yourself: aren't you more than ready to forgive one who you feel has hurt you in some way? You don't really want to hold a grudge, or condemn; you are really looking for a reason to forgive. You will eagerly accept almost any explanation; you will go to great lengths to find a reason to say, "Well, he didn't mean it that way . . . he has his troubles too, and maybe I misunderstood him after all."

Or turn the tables. Remember how often you have been forgiven, how often your failings and foibles and outright "sins" have been "redeemed" through the understanding and

155

loving tolerance of those around you. For almost any of us, life would be utterly hopeless if we had to "pay for" our mistakes of the past. But our friends and those who love us—even those with whom we associate on a rather impersonal basis—are in general quick, even eager, to forgive and forget.

(Of course there are a few individuals who seem to thrive on long-held grudges, who almost make hating a way of life . . . but they are so rare, so unusual, that they stand out. And of course there is always a reason why such people are the way they are.)

One of Jesus' most forceful instructions, because it seems at first glance so revolutionary, is that of the "second mile": "If any one strikes you on the right cheek, turn to him the other also; and if any one would sue you and take your coat, let him have your cloak as well; and if any one forces you to go one mile, go with him two miles."

Revolutionary? Yes . . . and even now, "turning the other cheek" is often used to describe meekness and humbleness, rather than power. But these words are so familiar to us that we accept them as part of the very core of Jesus' teaching. And most of us are a little uncomfortable, I think, when we read Paul's instructions to do good to our enemy, "for by so doing you will heap burning coals upon his head." We know instinctively that if we forgive another and return good for evil because in so doing we will punish our enemy, we are not gaining very much for ourself. (Even the parenthetical explanation given in "The Living New Testament" isn't very reassuring: "In other words, he will feel ashamed of himself for what he has done to you.") It is good to realize that the "coals of fire" notion is not Jesus'.

We usually use the phrase "human nature" to describe mankind's seamy side. Actually human nature is, by and large, good . . . it is simply a "down-to-earth" version of divine nature, applied to the people and circumstances of everyday life.

Our capacity for forgiveness, for giving others the privilege of a new beginning, is virtually unlimited . . . and the same is true of those to whom we look for understanding and kindness. We surely have taken to heart Jesus' words to Peter, in answer to the question as how often a brother should be forgiven: "I do not say to you seven times, but seventy times seven."

Sometimes when one is "down and out," bereft of hope and despondent, a well-meaning friend or counselor will advise the unfortunate one that he is his own master; that no one else has any power over him; that he can make a new beginning in spite of all opposition and criticism. This is true . . . but it isn't always a necessary piece of advice. Certainly I can begin again, regardless of what has happened, without the approval or support of anyone; but why should I, when I can almost certainly have the love and encouragement of a few (perhaps many) persons.

We underestimate the limitless reservoir of love and forgiveness to which we have access. Until we *are* in trouble, we seldom realize what a vast reserve of support and friendship and encouragement we have available. It may be trite to say, "You never know who your friends are until you're in trouble," but it is quite true . . . at least, you don't know just how strong and constant your friends are until you call on them in a time of crisis.

"All humanity is divided into two classes," said Frank Whitney, "those who despair, and those who have the courage to advance. Those

158

who believe that things of the world can defeat them and those who know that they have within them something that is undefeatable. Those who allow an early disappointment to dampen their spirits and those who use it as a stepping-stone. Those who let things master them and those who master things. Those who let circumstances shout 'Failure' to them and those who let their indwelling spirit cheer them on with 'Try again!' "

It was Annie Rix Militz who wrote that "forgiveness is not a sentiment but a power." Use this power by extending forgiveness to others—and tap the power by accepting it from others. "Today is the first day of the rest of your life," if you believe it.

Why not begin again . . . right now?

Printed U.S.A.

1 2 1 F-1 5 M-5 -7 3